Ranger Rick's NatureScope

WILD AND CRAFTY

National Wildlife Federation

LEARNING TRIANGLE PRESS

*Connecting
kids, parents, and teachers
through learning*

An imprint of McGraw-Hill

New York San Francisco Washington, D.C. Auckland Bogotá Caracas
Lisbon London Madrid Mexico City Milan Montreal New Delhi
San Juan Singapore Sydney Tokyo Toronto

Library of Congress Cataloging-in-Publication Data applied for

McGraw-Hill

A Division of The **McGraw·Hill** *Companies*

NATIONAL WILDLIFE FEDERATION®

1 2 3 4 5 6 7 8 9 JDL/JDL 9 0 3 2 1 0 9 8

ISBN 0-07-047112-6

NatureScope® was originally conceived by National Wildlife Federation's School Programs Editorial Staff, under the direction of Judy Braus, Editor. Special thanks to all of the Editorial Staff, Scientific, Educational Consultants and Contributors who brought this series of eighteen publications to life.

NATIONAL WILDLIFE FEDERATION EDITORIAL STAFF
Creative Services Manager: Sharon Schiliro
Editor, Ranger Rick® magazine: Gerry Bishop
Director, Classroom-related Programs: Margaret Tunstall
Contributors: Barbara Dondiego

McGRAW-HILL EDP STAFF
Acquisitions Editor: Judith Terrill-Breuer
Editorial Supervisor: Patricia V. Amoroso
Production Supervisor: Clare Stanley
Designer: York Production Services
Cover Design: David Saylor

RRNS

OTHER TITLES IN *RANGER RICK'S NATURESCOPE*

AMAZING MAMMALS, PART I
AMAZING MAMMALS, PART II
ASTRONOMY ADVENTURES
BIRDS, BIRDS, BIRDS
DIGGING INTO DINOSAURS
DISCOVERING DESERTS
DIVING INTO OCEANS
ENDANGERED SPECIES: WILD & RARE

GEOLOGY: THE ACTIVE EARTH
INCREDIBLE INSECTS
LET'S HEAR IT FOR HERPS
POLLUTION: PROBLEMS & SOLUTIONS
RAIN FORESTS: TROPICAL TREASURES
TREES ARE TERRIFIC!
WADING INTO WETLANDS
WILD ABOUT WEATHER

GOAL

Ranger Rick's NatureScope is a creative education series dedicated to inspiring in children an understanding and appreciation of the natural world while developing the skills they will need to make responsible decisions about the environment.

WILD AND CRAFTY

A Close-Up Look At
Wild And Crafty

Looking at the Table of Contents, you can see that Wild and Crafty contains a variety of creative crafts and a bibliography. Each of the crafts includes step-by-step directions and an illustration of the finished craft. The materials you'll need and a list of appropriate age groups are printed in the left-hand margin for easy reference. Each craft also includes some fun facts about the animal or subject featured in the craft, and a "Branching Out" section with suggestions for how to use the craft and ways to find out more about the subject.

Age Groups
The suggested age groups are: Primary (grades K-2), Intermediate (grades 3-5), and Advanced (6-8). But don't feel bound by the grade levels we suggest. You'll be able to adapt many of the crafts to fit your particular needs.

Craft Patterns
Many of the crafts have patterns for you to trace or copy. All of the patterns are drawn to size and don't need to be enlarged or reduced.

What's At The End
The final section, the *Bibliography*, lists a variety of craft books and includes an index to *NatureScope®* and *RangerRick®* crafts.

Table of Contents

Construct a zoetrope (ZO-ee-trope) and watch still pictures come to life.

___

Ages:
Advanced

Materials for one zoetrope:
- **copy of patterns on page 7**
- **oaktag or poster-board**
- **paper cup (12–16 oz.)**
- **sharp scissors**
- **compass**
- **pencil with an eraser (pencil should be slightly shorter than the paper cup)**
- **tape**
- **glue**

1. Cut apart the pattern page along the dashed line. Set the section with strips C and D aside for later.

2. Glue the section with pattern pieces A and B to a piece of oaktag or posterboard. (Spread a *thin* film of glue evenly over the entire back of the paper.) Let the glue dry, then cut out the two pattern pieces. (Don't forget to cut out the narrow slits along the top.)

3. Tape pattern pieces A and B together end to end to form a ring, making sure the black side faces out. Tape each tab to the inside of the ring as shown. Also tape the seams on the outside of the ring (see diagram 1).

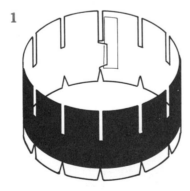

4. Bend the tabs around the bottom of the ring so that they face inward (see diagram 2).

5. Use a compass to draw a circle with a 4-inch diameter on a piece of oaktag or posterboard. (Push the compass point into the

paper to make a hole that you'll be able to find later.) Cut out the circle.

6. Drop the circle into the ring to form a base for the zoetrope and tape the tabs securely to the base as shown in diagram 2.

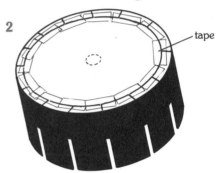

7. Push a pencil point down through the hole in the center of the base until just the eraser end is still showing (see diagram 3).

8. Put enough glue around the pencil to hold it in place. Let dry.

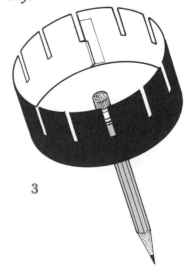

Action

9. Cut out strips C and D from the section of the pattern page you set aside earlier. Tape the strips together end to end to form a loop, making sure the pictures face *inside* (see diagram 4). Be sure to tape the tabs on the outside of the loop. Also tape the seams on the inside. Put the picture loop inside the frame you made earlier so that it rests evenly on the base.

(continued next page)

4

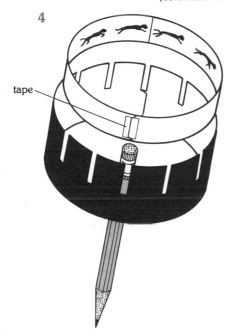

tape

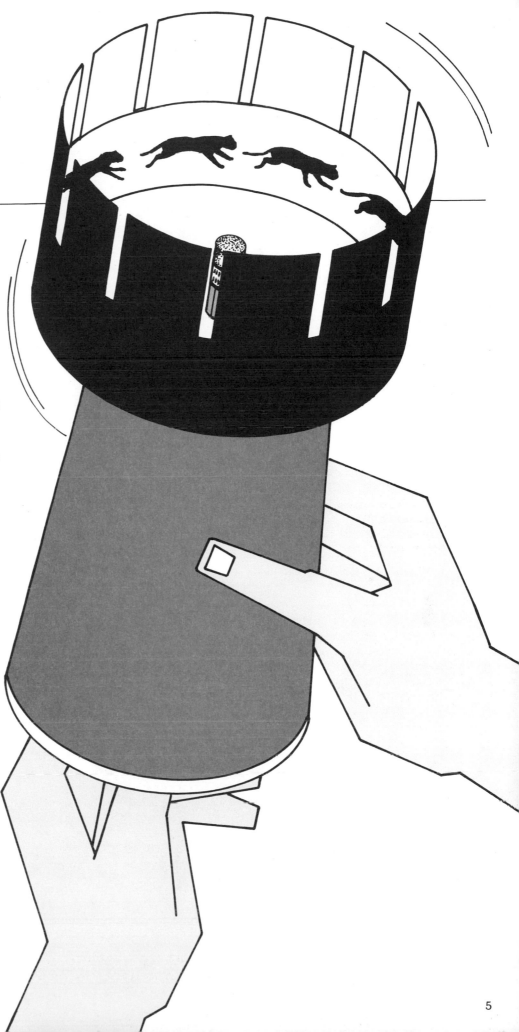

10. Turn the paper cup upside down. Poke the pencil that's in the base into the center of the cup's bottom and push until the base is resting on the cup. Turn the pencil around in the cup's hole until it moves freely.

11. Hold the cup with one hand so that the top of the completed zoetrope is at eye level. Reach inside the cup with the other hand and twirl the pencil. As you look through the slits in the spinning zoetrope, you'll be able to see the cat spring into action!

Branching Out

- Find out about the history of motion pictures, using these key words, names, and titles to guide your research: Thomas A. Edison, celluloid, kinetoscope, Georges Méliès, "The Great Train Robbery," nickelodeon, Hollywood, D.W. Griffith, the Keystone Cops, "The Jazz Singer."
- See page 8 of *Nature-Scope—Birds, Birds, Birds!* for instructions on how to make a "flip-book" that shows a bird flying.

This craft is adapted with permission from *The Metropolitan Museum of Art Activity Book* by Osa Brown, published by Random House, Inc., copyright 1983.

Fun Facts

- The zoetrope was sold as a toy when it was first invented in the mid-1800s.

- The first photographs to successfully record motion were taken of a galloping horse by Eadweard Muybridge in 1887.

- A motion picture is made up of thousands of separate pictures, or **frames,** each of which is flashed on the screen for just 1/24 of a second.

- It may take more than a million separate drawings to create a feature-length motion picture cartoon.

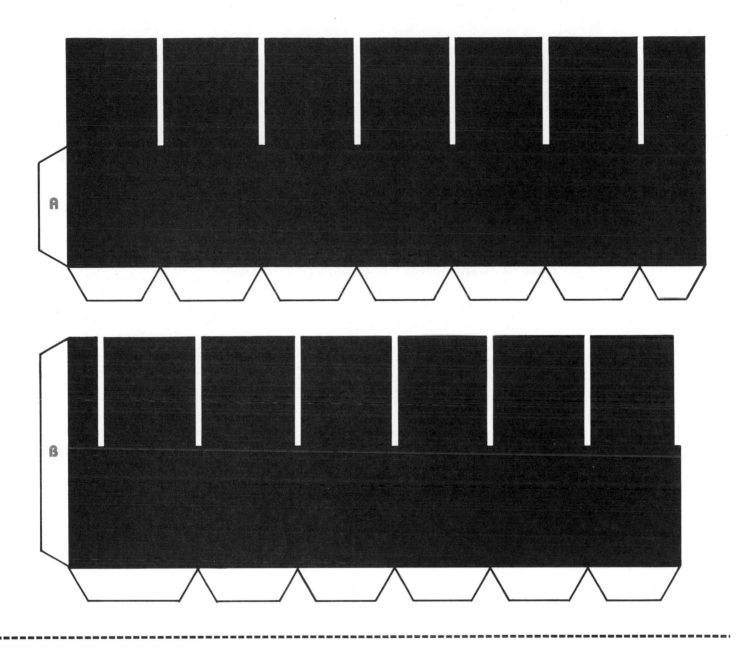

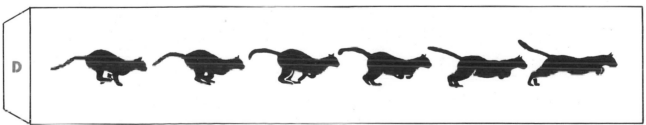

copy these patterns

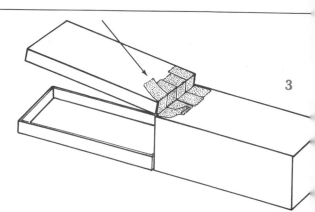

Make a shoebox alligator with jaws that open and close.

Ages:
Intermediate and Advanced

Materials for one alligator:
- *copy of patterns on page 11*
- *shoeboxes (two lids and one bottom)*
- *ruler*
- *string*
- *masking tape*
- *glue*
- *sharp scissors*
- *yardstick*
- *construction paper*
- *three paper fasteners*
- *paint and paintbrush*
- *pushpin*
- *cardboard egg carton*
- *cardboard*

1. Using a pair of sharp scissors, poke two holes in the rim of one of the short sides of a shoebox lid (see diagram 1).

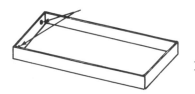

1

2. Turn a shoebox over so the opening is facing down. Line up the lid (with the inside facing up) and the box end to end and poke two holes in the box the same distance apart as those in the lid. Attach the lid to the box by pushing a paper fastener through each hole in the lid and then through each hole in the box (see diagram 2). Secure the paper fasteners.

3. To make the upper jaw of the alligator, tape a second lid (with the inside facing down) to the top of the box. The tape should form a hinge (see diagram 3).

4. To make the alligator's tail, cut two triangles out of cardboard. Each triangle should be about 19 inches long, with a base as wide as the shoebox bottom.

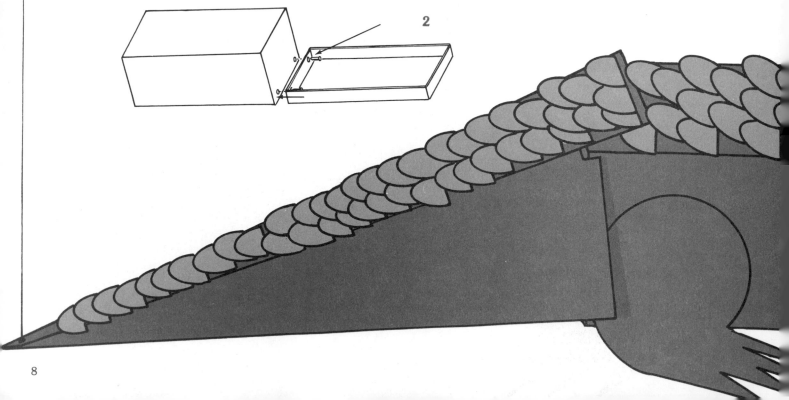

Alligator

Cut the two corners off the base of *one* of the triangles (see diagram 4).

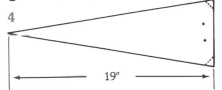

4

19″

5. Use scissors to poke two small holes in the base of each triangle. The holes should be about ¾ inch from the base of the triangle and 1½ inches apart.

6. Poke two small holes in the bottom of the shoebox. The holes should be about ¾ inch from the end of the box and the same distance apart as those in the triangles.

7. Lay the triangle without the clipped corners on the box bottom so that the holes in the triangle and box bottom are lined up. Thread an 18-inch piece of string through both sets of holes (see diagram 5). Then thread the string through the holes in the triangle with the clipped corners and tie the two ends of the string loosely together (see diagram 6 on next page).

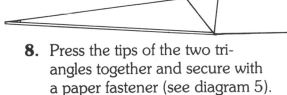

5

8. Press the tips of the two triangles together and secure with a paper fastener (see diagram 5).

(continued next page)

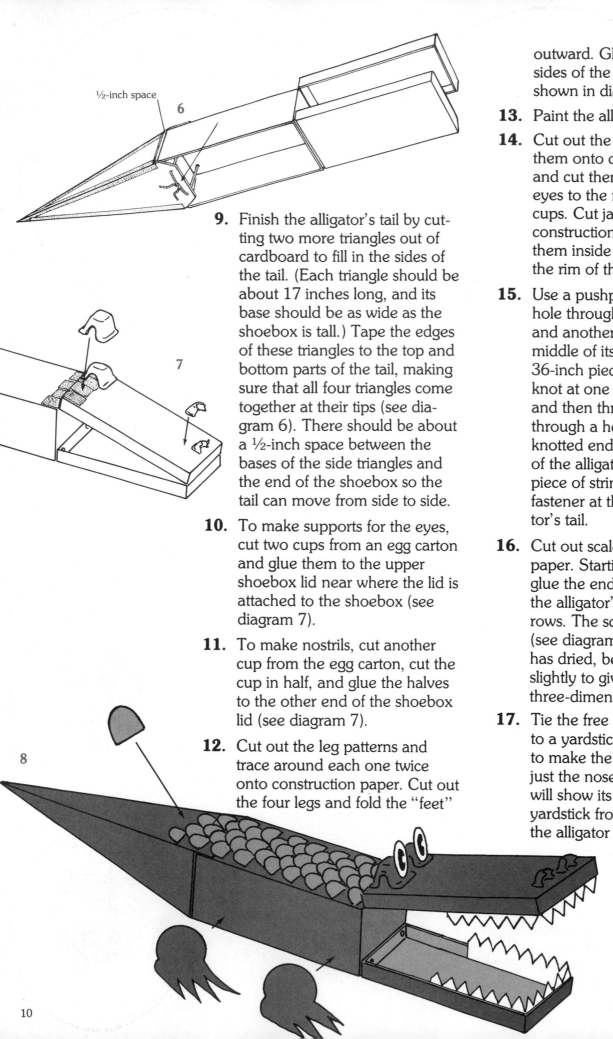

½-inch space

6

7

8

9. Finish the alligator's tail by cutting two more triangles out of cardboard to fill in the sides of the tail. (Each triangle should be about 17 inches long, and its base should be as wide as the shoebox is tall.) Tape the edges of these triangles to the top and bottom parts of the tail, making sure that all four triangles come together at their tips (see diagram 6). There should be about a ½-inch space between the bases of the side triangles and the end of the shoebox so the tail can move from side to side.

10. To make supports for the eyes, cut two cups from an egg carton and glue them to the upper shoebox lid near where the lid is attached to the shoebox (see diagram 7).

11. To make nostrils, cut another cup from the egg carton, cut the cup in half, and glue the halves to the other end of the shoebox lid (see diagram 7).

12. Cut out the leg patterns and trace around each one twice onto construction paper. Cut out the four legs and fold the "feet"

outward. Glue the legs to the sides of the alligator's body as shown in diagram 8.

13. Paint the alligator and let dry.

14. Cut out the eye patterns, glue them onto construction paper, and cut them out. Then glue the eyes to the fronts of the egg cups. Cut jagged teeth out of construction paper and glue them inside the mouth, along the rim of the shoebox lids.

15. Use a pushpin to poke one hole through the alligator's nose and another hole through the middle of its back. Cut three 36-inch pieces of string. Tie a knot at one end of two strings and then thread each piece through a hole so that the knotted end is on the underside of the alligator. Tie the third piece of string around the paper fastener at the tip of the alligator's tail.

16. Cut out scales from construction paper. Starting behind the head, glue the ends of the scales along the alligator's back and tail in rows. The scales should overlap (see diagram 8). After the glue has dried, bend the scales up slightly to give them a more three-dimensional look.

17. Tie the free end of each string to a yardstick. Lift the yardstick to make the alligator walk. Lift just the nose and the alligator will show its teeth. Move the yardstick from side to side and the alligator will wave its tail.

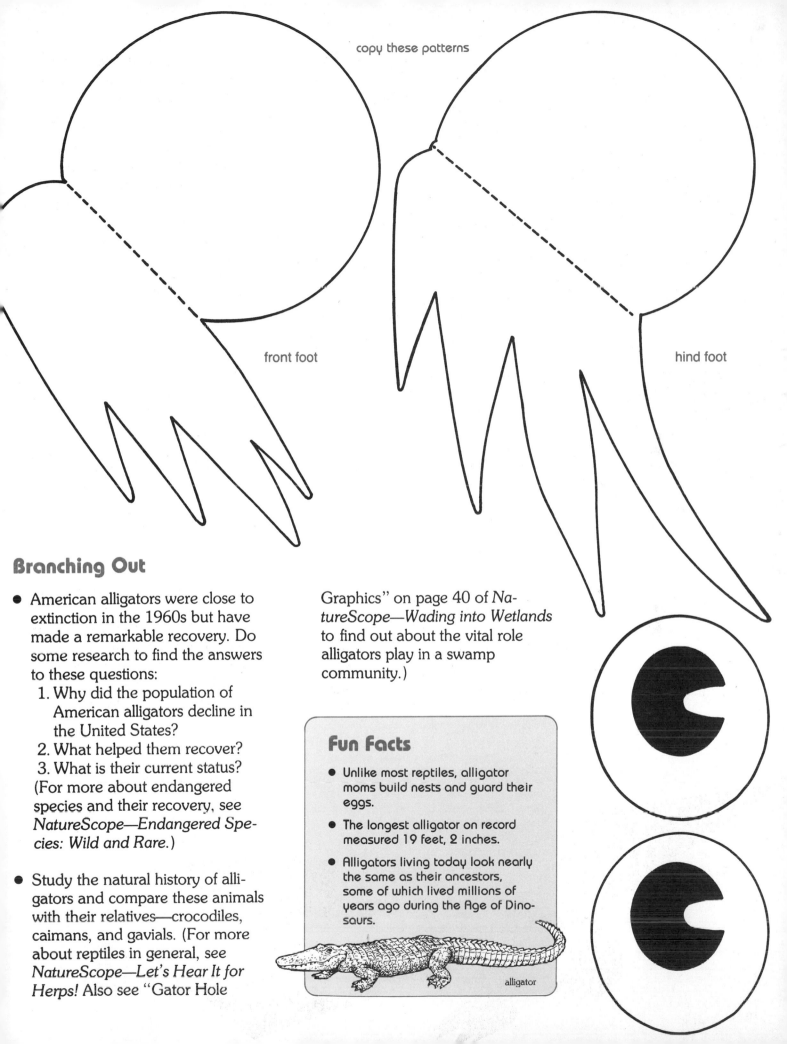

front foot

hind foot

Branching Out

- American alligators were close to extinction in the 1960s but have made a remarkable recovery. Do some research to find the answers to these questions:
  1. Why did the population of American alligators decline in the United States?
  2. What helped them recover?
  3. What is their current status?
  (For more about endangered species and their recovery, see *NatureScope—Endangered Species: Wild and Rare*.)

- Study the natural history of alligators and compare these animals with their relatives—crocodiles, caimans, and gavials. (For more about reptiles in general, see *NatureScope—Let's Hear It for Herps!* Also see "Gator Hole

Graphics" on page 40 of *NatureScope—Wading into Wetlands* to find out about the vital role alligators play in a swamp community.)

Fun Facts

- Unlike most reptiles, alligator moms build nests and guard their eggs.

- The longest alligator on record measured 19 feet, 2 inches.

- Alligators living today look nearly the same as their ancestors, some of which lived millions of years ago during the Age of Dinosaurs.

alligator

Make an anteater puppet with a tongue that zaps!

Ages:
Intermediate

Materials for one puppet:
- *construction paper*
- *scissors*
- *tape*
- *ruler*
- *glue*
- *sock*
- *long pipe cleaner*
- *12-inch piece of flexible wire (about 22 gauge)*
- *stapler*

1. Cut a 9-inch wedge out of construction paper. Trim the point as shown.

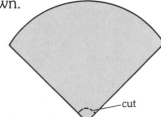

2. To make the anteater's head, roll the wedge into a cone and tape the edges together. Make sure you leave a small opening at the tip of the cone (see diagram).

tape

3. Cut out construction paper ears and eyes and glue them in place on the cone.

4. Hold a 12-inch piece of wire in your hand and pull a sock over that hand. Poke the end of the wire through the toe of the sock. Then carefully remove your hand from the sock and twist the end of the wire with the end of a pipe cleaner, outside the sock as shown.

twist pipe cleaner and wire together

5. Insert the sock about a third of the way into the cone and staple the sock to the cone (see diagram).

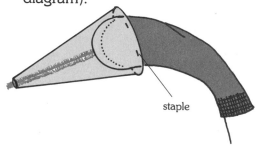

staple

6. Put one hand into the sock and manipulate the wire with your other hand to move the anteater's pipe cleaner tongue in and out.

Fun Facts

- Anteaters live in southern Mexico and in Central and South America.

- There are four species of anteaters. The smallest species, the silky anteater, measures a foot from head to tail and weighs about 6 ounces. The largest species, the giant anteater, can reach a length of 7 feet and weigh more than 80 pounds.

- Anteaters feed mostly on ants and termites. The giant anteater can extend its sticky tongue 24 inches to zap its prey.

giant anteater

Zapper

Branching Out

- Use your imagination to come up with stories that explain how ant-eaters, platypuses, numbats, and other animals acquired their unusual adaptations. See "Fact and Fancy" on page 70 of *NatureScope—Amazing Mammals II.*

- Play a game in which partners take turns describing and drawing some unusual "mystery mammals," such as anteaters. See "Oddball Options" on page 68 of *NatureScope— Amazing Mammals II.*

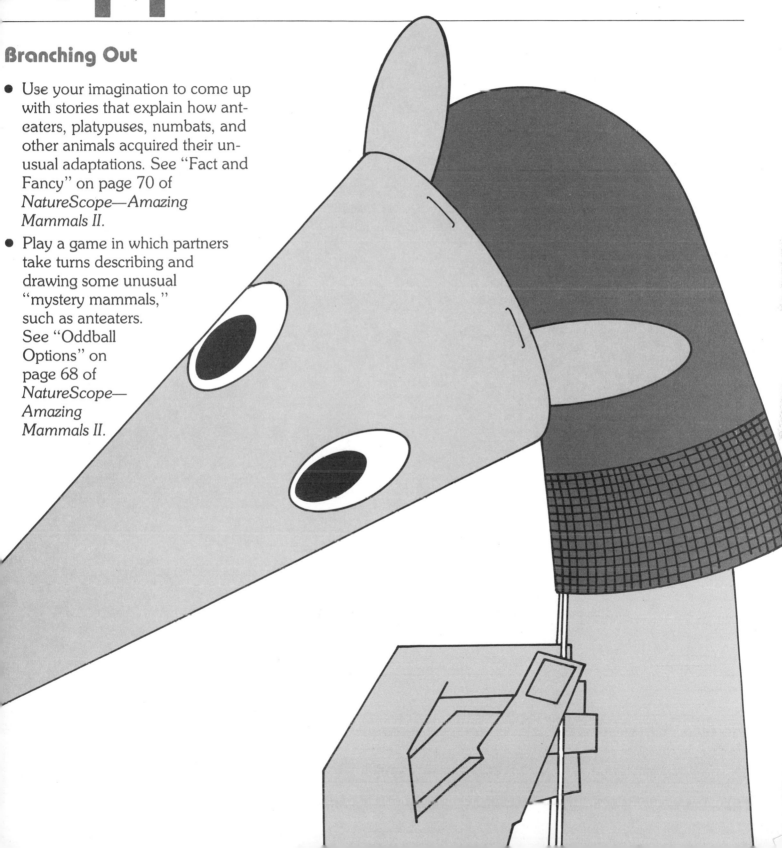

Birds of a Feather

Create a nest of baby birds.

Ages:
Primary

Materials for one nest:
- *copy of patterns below*
- *construction paper*
- *glue*
- *scissors*
- *pencil*
- *ruler*

1. Cut out the pattern pieces and trace around them on construction paper. Mix and match the pattern pieces to create several different-looking birds. Then glue a beak, a tail, and wings in place on each bird's body and let dry.

2. Make a nest by cutting out a half circle with a 6-inch diameter. Glue small strips of construction paper grass or twigs to the nest.

3. Turn the nest over. Put a thin line of glue along the curved edge, but not across the straight edge. Glue the nest to a piece of construction paper and let dry.

4. Write the names of family members, classmates, or friends on the different birds and slide each bird into the nest "pocket."

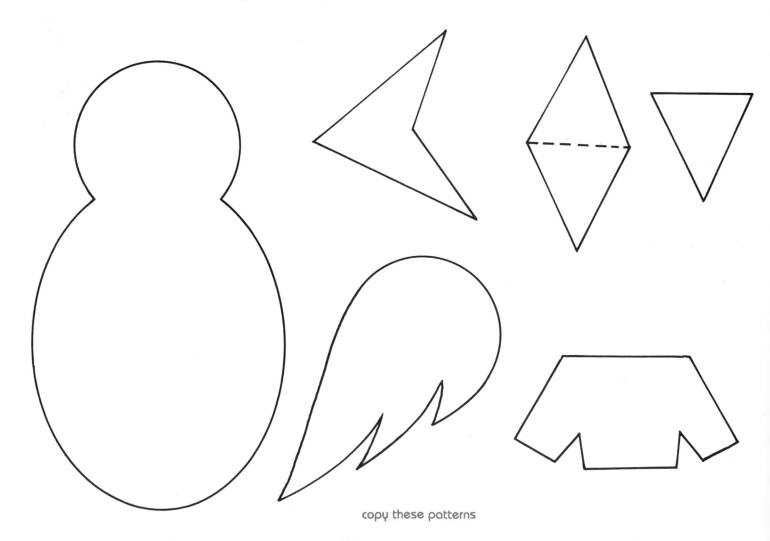

copy these patterns

Branching Out

- Make a bulletin board bird nest. Cut out a nest large enough to fit the size of the board and then staple it in place around the curved edge only. Have each member of a group or class make a bird to put in the nest.

- Take a walk to observe birds. If you see a bird's nest, watch it awhile from a distance to find out if anything is going on. For example, are the parents building the nest, feeding babies in the nest, or sitting on eggs?

- Try to make your own nest out of natural materials. See "House Hunting" on page 22 of *NatureScope— Birds, Birds, Birds!* for instructions.

Fun Facts

- Hummingbirds build the smallest-known nests. Some hummingbird nests are no more than an inch wide and an inch deep.

- Bald eagles build some of the biggest nests in North America. One eagle nest was about 9 feet wide and 20 feet deep.

- Some birds don't build nests at all. Many seabirds lay their eggs on bare rock. Fairy terns lay their single eggs in the fork of a tree branch. And cowbirds and European cuckoos lay their eggs in the nests of other birds.

- People in Asia make bird's nest soup out of the dried nests of swiftlets. The nests are made entirely of the birds' saliva.

fairy tern

Caterpillar

Make an accordion-folded paper caterpillar.

Ages:
Primary

Materials for one caterpillar:
- *construction paper*
- *tape or glue*
- *scissors*
- *ruler*
- *crayons or markers*

1. Cut two circles, each 3½ inches in diameter, out of construction paper. The circles will be the caterpillar's front and back ends.

2. Cut a 3½ × 12-inch rectangle out of construction paper. This will be the caterpillar's body.

3. Use crayons or markers to decorate the caterpillar's body. Draw its eyes and mouth on one of the circles.

4. Make accordion folds, each about 1 inch wide, along the length of the body.

5. Tape or glue the caterpillar face to one end of the body and the other circle to the back end of the body.

6. You can also tape or glue on construction paper "horns" or spines.

Branching Out

- Design other accordion animals. For example, you can make an accordion armadillo, raccoon, cat, or fox out of construction paper.
- Use finger movements to review

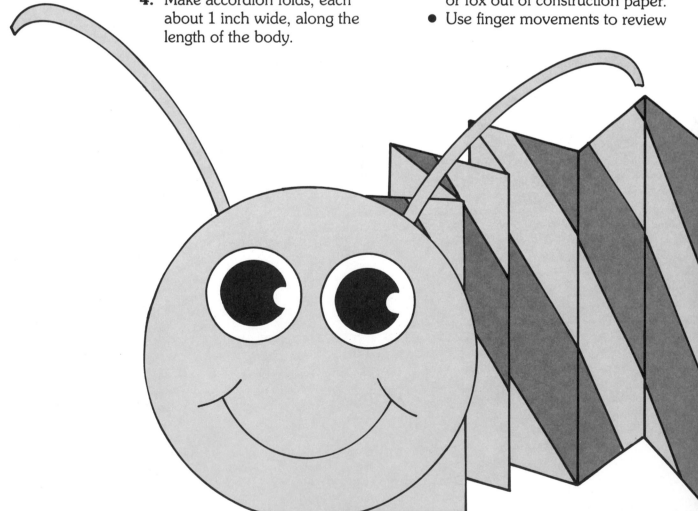

Pal

the life cycle of a butterfly. See "Caterpillar Finger Play" on page 19 of *NatureScope—Incredible Insects.*

- Take a walk to look for different kinds of caterpillars.
- For some tips on how to raise caterpillars indoors, see "Caterpillar Capers" on page 21 of *NatureScope—Incredible Insects.* Then try the "Caterpillar Caper Maze" on page 23 of the same issue.

Fun Facts

monarch caterpillar

- Moths and butterflies go through four life stages: egg, larva, pupa, and adult. A caterpillar is the larval stage.

- Caterpillars munch on leaves and other plant parts with their strong, chewing jaws. Some "picky" caterpillars eat only one kind of plant.

- In North America, the smallest caterpillars are less than ¼ inch long. But the biggest caterpillars can get to be nearly 6 inches long.

- Some caterpillars have smooth skin. Others have hairs, spines, or fleshy "horns" on their bodies.

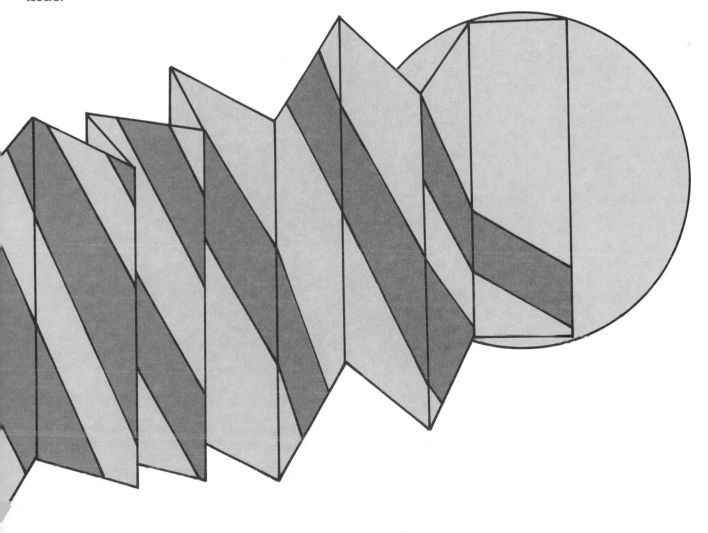

Climbing Critters

Ages:
Intermediate

Materials:
- **crayons or markers**
- **scissors**
- **glue**
- **ruler**

To make a spider:
- **copy of patterns
  below**
- **thin cardboard**
- **yarn**
- **pencil**
- **four short pipe
  cleaners**
- **drinking straw (paper
  straws work best)**
- **tape**

To make a monkey:
- **copy of patterns on
  page 21**
- **oaktag or poster-
  board**
- **1-yard piece of string**
- **pushpin**

Spider in a Web

1. Color the spider body pattern.
   Glue the body and web patterns
   onto thin cardboard and cut them
   out. (You may want to glue
   pieces of yarn onto the web pattern to make it look three-
   dimensional.)

2. Cut two ½-inch pieces from a
   drinking straw. Glue the pieces

onto the underside of the spider
body as shown. If you're using a
plastic straw, tape the straw pieces
to the cardboard spider's body to
make sure they stick.

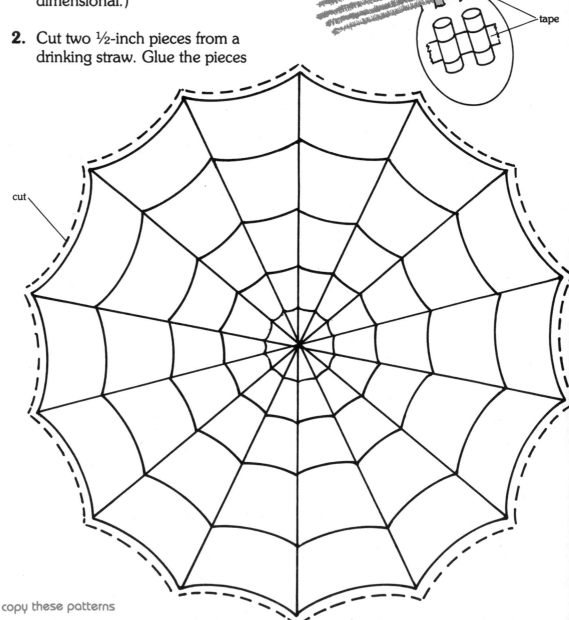

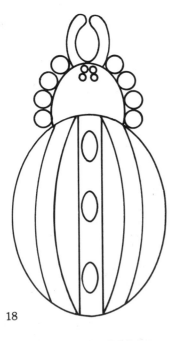

cut

copy these patterns

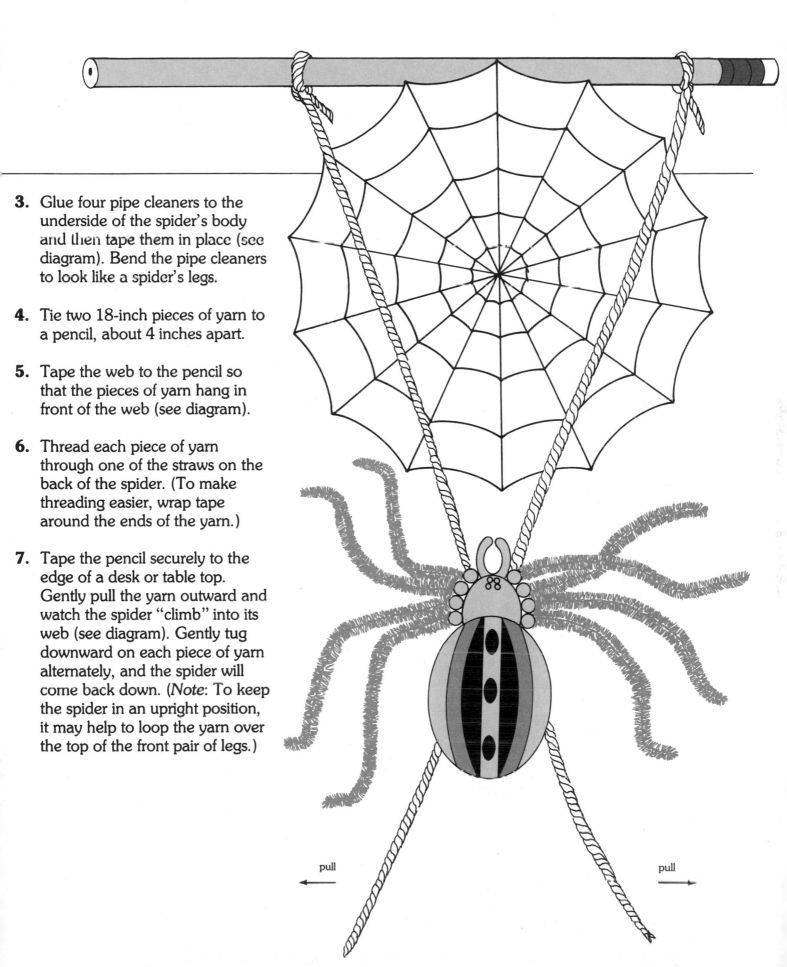

3. Glue four pipe cleaners to the underside of the spider's body and then tape them in place (see diagram). Bend the pipe cleaners to look like a spider's legs.

4. Tie two 18-inch pieces of yarn to a pencil, about 4 inches apart.

5. Tape the web to the pencil so that the pieces of yarn hang in front of the web (see diagram).

6. Thread each piece of yarn through one of the straws on the back of the spider. (To make threading easier, wrap tape around the ends of the yarn.)

7. Tape the pencil securely to the edge of a desk or table top. Gently pull the yarn outward and watch the spider "climb" into its web (see diagram). Gently tug downward on each piece of yarn alternately, and the spider will come back down. (*Note*: To keep the spider in an upright position, it may help to loop the yarn over the top of the front pair of legs.)

pull

pull

Monkey up a Tree

1. Color the monkey patterns and cut them out.

2. Glue one of the monkey patterns onto a piece of oaktag or posterboard. (Use a thin film of glue spread evenly across the entire back of the pattern.) Let dry and then cut out the piece. Glue the other pattern to the back side of this piece and let dry.

3. Use a pushpin to poke holes through the circles on the monkey's hand and foot. Turn the pushpin around in the holes to make them just big enough to thread string through.

4. Double a 1-yard piece of string and thread the loop end through the hole in the foot and then through the hole in the hand (see diagram). You may need to use a pencil point to enlarge the holes a bit and to push the string through them.

5. Tie a knot at each free end of the string. The knots should be big enough to keep the ends of the string from slipping through the hole in the foot.

6. Put the loop over a doorknob and start the monkey at the bottom of the string. Make the monkey climb by pulling one string. Pull the other string to make it go down. If you keep pulling the string, the monkey will start back up.

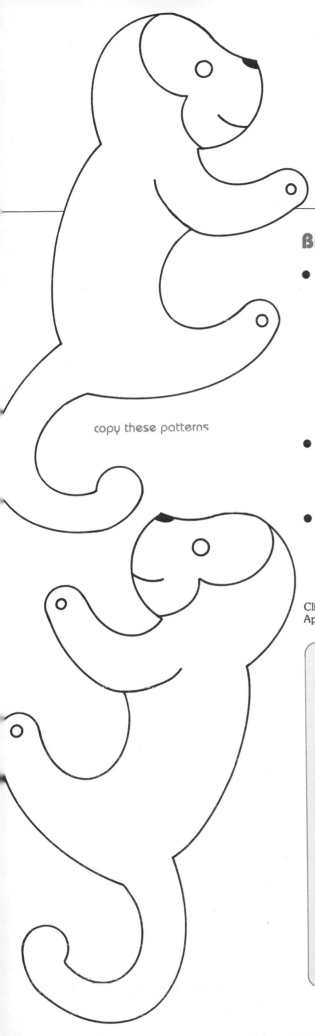

copy these patterns

Branching Out

- Compare monkeys with some other animals that climb trees. For example, find out how tree frogs, raccoons, squirrels, snakes, and caterpillars are adapted for climbing. (For more information about monkeys and their adaptations, see pages 3–5 of *NatureScope—Amazing Mammals II.*)
- Learn about the differences between spiders and insects. See "Eight Legs or Six?" on page 11 of *NatureScope—Incredible Insects.*
- Look in a field guide to find out what kinds of web-spinning spiders live in your area and then take a walk to find some webs.

Climbing monkey craft adapted from *Ranger Rick,* April 1967.

spider monkey

Fun Facts

- Many monkeys spend almost all their time in trees. Their grasping fingers and/or toes really come in "handy" when they climb.

- Some monkeys have grasping, or **prehensile,** tails that help them hang on to branches.

- The spider in this craft is an orb weaver. Orb weavers get their name from the round webs they usually spin.

- Many spiders have an oily coating on their legs that helps keep them from sticking to their webs.

Flutter

Make a colorful butter-fly kite.

Ages:
Primary

Materials for one kite:
- *copy of patterns below*
- *tissue paper*
- *two drinking straws (paper straws work best)*
- *glue*
- *tape*
- *2-foot piece of string*
- *markers*
- *scissors*

1. Trace around the kite pattern onto a piece of tissue paper and cut it out. (Or you can just cut out and use the kite pattern piece instead of using tissue paper.)

2. Cut out the butterfly body and glue it to the middle of the kite.

3. Use markers to decorate the kite like a butterfly. The colors will show through both sides of the tissue paper wings.

4. Lay one end of a 2-foot piece of string across the middle of the kite as shown. Make sure the end of

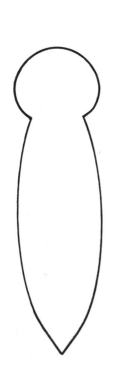

copy these patterns

22

Kite

the string extends beyond the kite's center to the edge of the wing (see diagram).

5. Glue two straws onto the kite, crossing them in the middle to form an "X" on top of the string. Let dry. *Note:* If you're using plastic straws, tape them in place at each corner and in the middle where they cross.

6. Tie the string in a knot around the straws.

7. Hold onto the long end of the string and run with the kite. It will follow along behind you like a fluttering butterfly.

Butterfly kite by Pamela Wong. Adapted from *Ranger Rick,* June 1979.

Branching Out

● See "Moths vs Butterflies" on page 6 of *NatureScope—Incredible Insects Discovery Pac* for a story that describes the differences between moths and butterflies.
● Take a butterfly and moth hike to see these insects up close.

Queen Alexandra birdwing butterfly

Fun Facts

● Most butterflies feed on nectar.

● The Queen Alexandra birdwing butterfly has a wingspan of nearly a foot and is the largest butterfly in the world. These huge insects have always been rare, but are now endangered because of overcollecting and habitat loss.

● The western pygmy blue, one of the smallest butterflies in the world, has a wingspan of less than ½ inch.

● Butterfly wings are covered with thousands of tiny, powdery scales that give the wings their color.

Foxy Flapper

Make a model of a flying fox (a type of bat) with wings that flap.

Ages:
Advanced

Materials for one bat:
- **copy of patterns on pages 26 and 27**
- **thin cardboard**
- **pencil**
- **ruler**
- **scissors**
- **glue**
- **string**
- **craft stick**
- **tape**
- **pushpin**
- **markers, crayons, or paint and paintbrush**

1. Cut out the patterns for the bat's body and wings. Trace two of each pattern onto thin cardboard and cut them out. Draw a line along the bottom of each wing, about ½ inch from the edge (see pattern on page 27). Score along the lines and then bend these tabs back and forth. (The tabs will act as hinges for the wings.) Also cut out 18 half-inch cardboard squares.

2. On one of the bat body pieces, glue a cardboard square to each of the six places marked as stars in diagram 1. Glue two more squares on top of each of these.

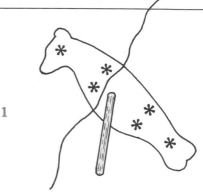

1

3. Glue a craft stick onto the body piece as shown. Let dry.

4. Cut an 18-inch piece of string and lay it across the body between the four middle squares (see diagram 1). There should be an equal amount of string on each side of the bat's body.

(continued on page 26)

Fun Facts

- Flying foxes—named for their fox-like faces—are the largest bats in the world. Some have wingspans that stretch nearly 6 feet!

- More than 30 different kinds of flying foxes live in Southeast Asia, Africa, and Australia, and on islands in the South Pacific. In some of these areas, flying foxes are endangered.

- Unlike many bats, which prey on insects, flying foxes eat fruit, nectar, and pollen. And instead of using echolocation, these big bats rely on their keen eyesight to help them find food.

flying fox

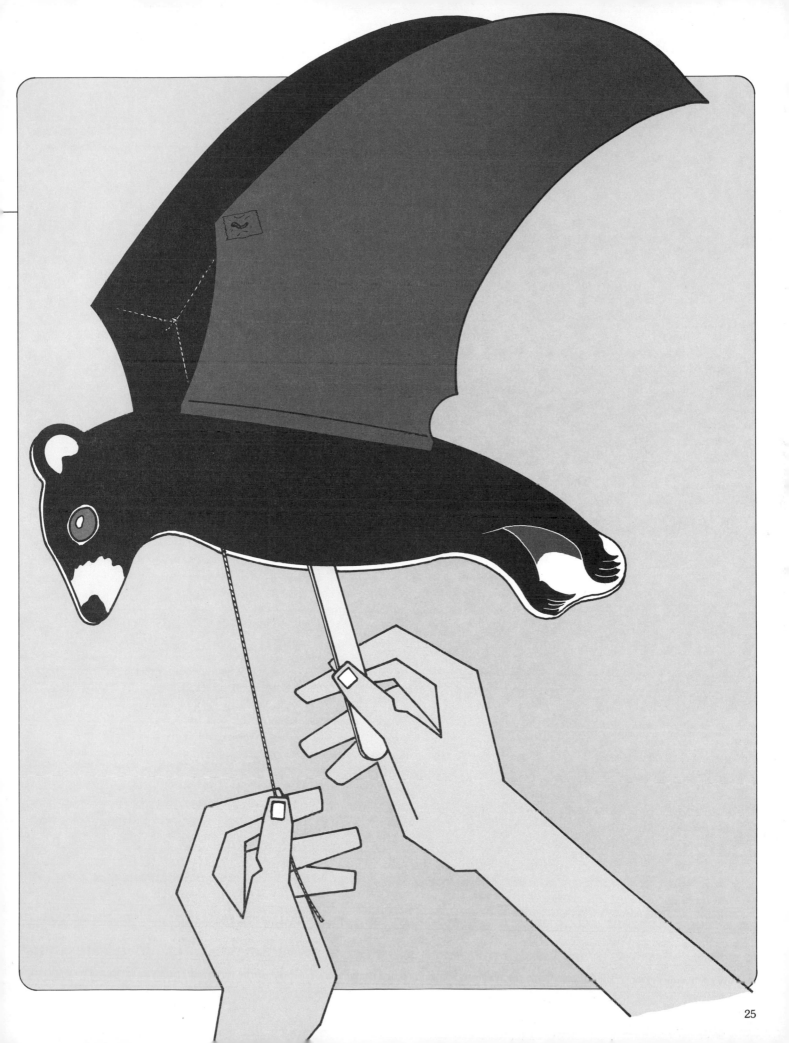

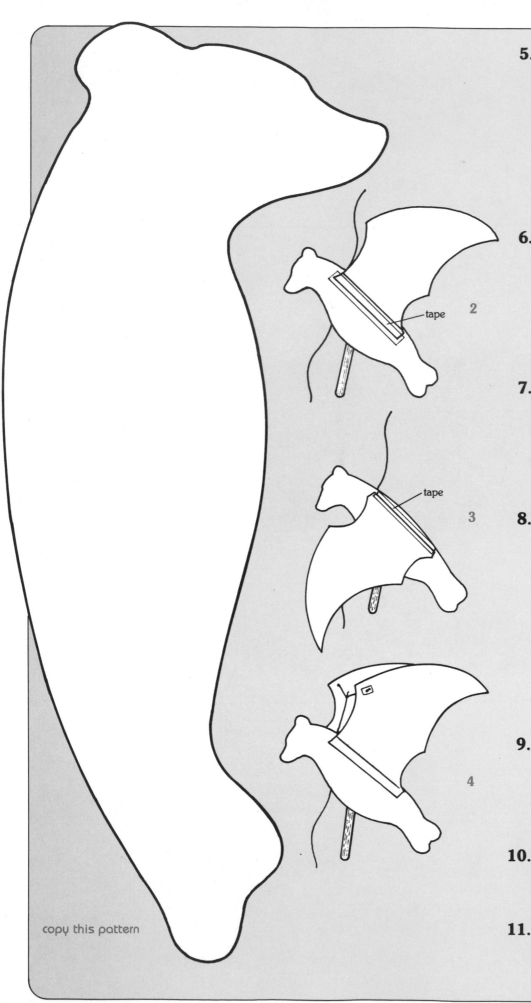

tape 2

tape

3

4

copy this pattern

5. Place a dot of glue on each of the cardboard squares and on the craft stick and then put the two halves of the bat's body together. Be sure to keep the halves of the body lined up. The string should remain between the body halves, but be careful not to get any glue on it. Let dry.

6. To attach a wing, lay the bat on one side. With the wing up, glue the back of the tab onto the body, about ½ inch from the top of the bat's back (see diagram 2). Then tape over the tab to hold it securely.

7. Once the wing is in place, bend it down and reinforce the hinge by taping it to the body along the seam (see diagram 3). Then turn the bat over and attach the second wing in the same way.

8. Use a pushpin to make a hole in each wing in the spot marked on the pattern. (Turn the pushpin around in the holes to make them just big enough to thread string through.) Then cut an 8-inch piece of string and thread the ends through the holes on top of the wings. Tape about ½ inch of string to the underside of each wing (see diagram 4).

9. Tie the end of the string running through the top of the bat's body to the *center* of the string connecting the wings (see diagram 4).

10. Use watercolors, poster paints, markers, or crayons to color the flying fox.

11. Hold the craft stick and pull the bottom of the long string to make the bat flap its wings.

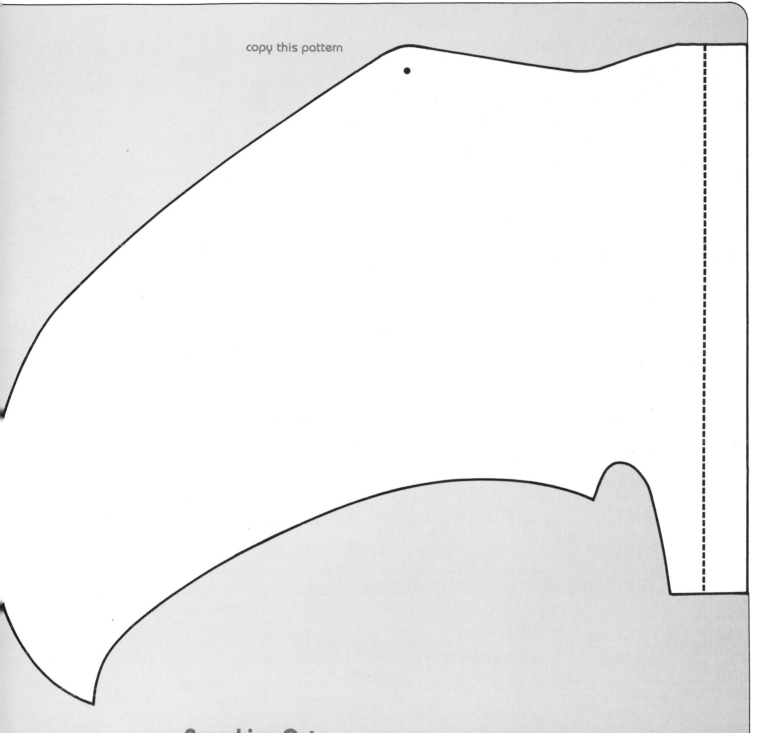

copy this pattern

Branching Out

- Find out how much you know about bats by trying the bat trivia quiz and by comparing two bat poems in "A Bat Like That" on page 36 of *NatureScope—Amazing Mammals II*.
- Flying foxes don't rely on echolocation to find food, but many other kinds of bats do. See "Ears in the Dark" on page 39 of *NatureScope—*

Amazing Mammals II to find out how scientists learned about bat echolocation.
- For more information on bats, see pages 33–34 of *NatureScope— Amazing Mammals II*. And for information on why flying foxes are endangered, see pages 42 and 46 of *NatureScope—Endangered Species: Wild and Rare.*

Octo-Puppet

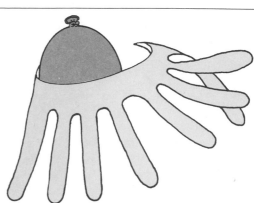

Make an octopus puppet.

Ages:
Primary and Intermediate

Materials for one puppet:
- small, round balloon
- gift wrap
- scissors
- ruler
- construction paper
- string
- two 1-foot wooden dowels or rulers
- tape

1. To make an octopus head, blow up a balloon and tie a knot in the end.

2. Use the diagram below as a guide to cut a strip of eight arms out of gift wrap. (The strip should be about the same length as the balloon's circumference.)

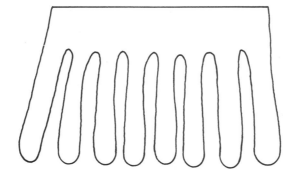

3. Wrap the strip of arms around the balloon, making sure that the knot in the balloon is at the top of the head. Tape the strip in place.

4. Cut out two eyes and a mouth from construction paper and tape them onto the puppet.

5. To make a crosspiece for manipulating the puppet, cross two 1-foot dowels or rulers in the middle and tie or tape them together.

6. Tie one end of an 18-inch piece of string to the knot on top of the balloon and tie the other end to the middle of the crosspiece.

7. Cut eight more pieces of string of varying lengths (22–32 inches). Tape one end of each piece of string to the tip of an arm and tie the other end to a dowel. Each dowel should have four arms attached to it by string—two on each side. *Hint:* Have a friend hold up the crosspiece as you tie so you don't get the strings crossed and tangled.

octopus

Fun Facts

- An octopus can have about 240 sensory suction cups on each of its 8 arms. It uses these suckers to grab and hold prey, to draw food toward its mouth, and to pull itself along rocky ocean bottoms.

- The eyes of a giant Pacific octopus can be as large as oranges.

- Many scientists think that after marine mammals, octopuses are the most intelligent creatures in the sea.

- An octopus changes colors when it's alarmed. It can also change colors to camouflage itself or to attract prey or a mate.

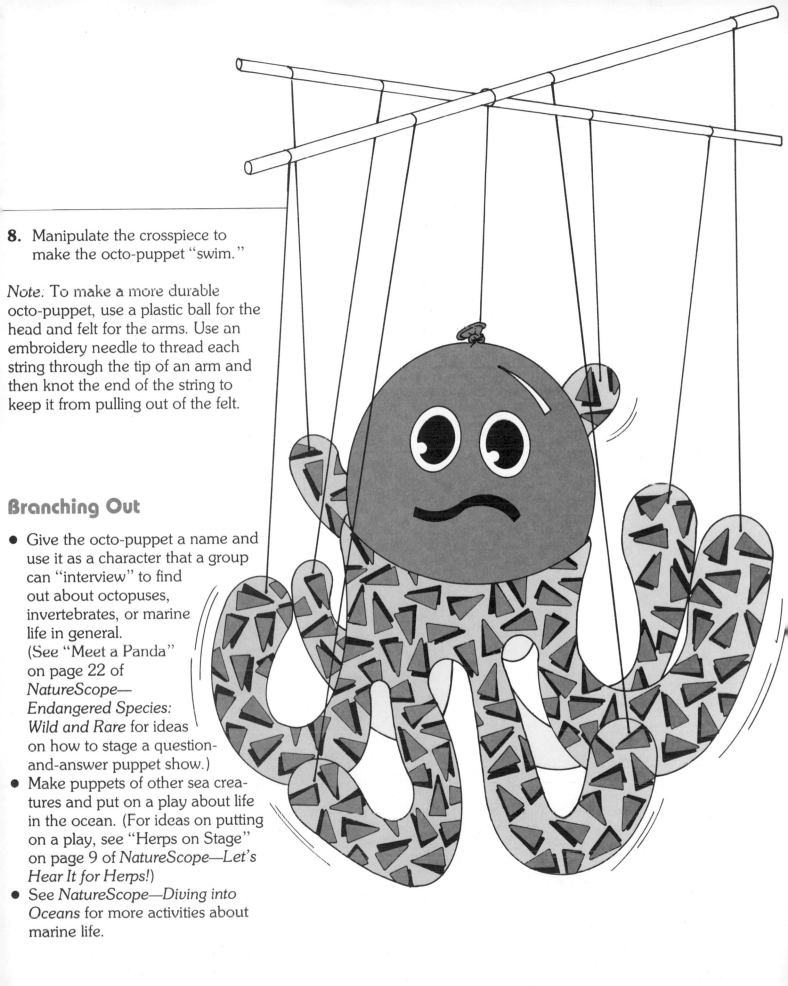

8. Manipulate the crosspiece to make the octo-puppet "swim."

Note: To make a more durable octo-puppet, use a plastic ball for the head and felt for the arms. Use an embroidery needle to thread each string through the tip of an arm and then knot the end of the string to keep it from pulling out of the felt.

Branching Out

- Give the octo-puppet a name and use it as a character that a group can "interview" to find out about octopuses, invertebrates, or marine life in general. (See "Meet a Panda" on page 22 of *NatureScope—Endangered Species: Wild and Rare* for ideas on how to stage a question-and-answer puppet show.)
- Make puppets of other sea creatures and put on a play about life in the ocean. (For ideas on putting on a play, see "Herps on Stage" on page 9 of *NatureScope—Let's Hear It for Herps!*)
- See *NatureScope—Diving into Oceans* for more activities about marine life.

29

Paper Puffer.

Cut out a paper porcupinefish that really puffs up.

Ages:
Advanced

Materials for one fish:
- **copy of patterns on page 33**
- **three sheets of plain white paper (8½ × 11")**
- **sharp scissors**
- **small, round balloon**
- **tape**
- **ruler**
- **stapler**

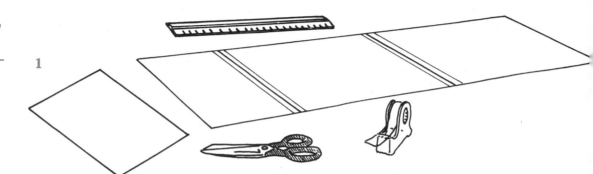

1

1. Tape three sheets of 8½ × 11" paper together end to end. Trim the length to 24 inches (see diagram 1).

2. Make 1-inch fan folds along the entire length of the paper. You should end up with about 24 folds (see diagram 2).

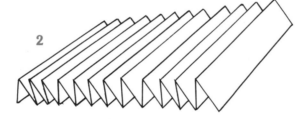

2

3. Tape the ends of the folded paper together, forming a pleated tube. The two ends should come together in a "hill" fold (see diagram 3). If they don't, trim off the extra paper before taping.

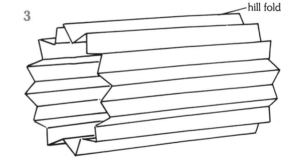

3

hill fold

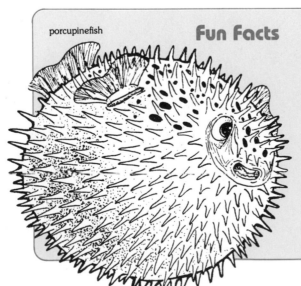

porcupinefish

Fun Facts

- When threatened, the spine-covered porcupinefish can expand into a prickly puff ball to discourage predators.

- If a predator gobbles up a porcupinefish, the porcupinefish can inflate right inside the predator's mouth, forcing the bigger fish to spit out the prickly mouthful.

- Porcupinefish and their relatives, puffers, puff up by swallowing water or, if they're out of the water, by swallowing air.

4. Fold the pleats back together so that all the hill folds are on one side and a "spine" runs along the other (see diagram 4).

4

5. Cut triangular notches about ½ inch deep through all layers on the hill-fold side of the paper (see diagram 5). Leave ½ inch between notches.

(continued next page)

5

6. Cut slits *no deeper* than ½ inch along the spine side, *in between* the notches (see diagram 6).

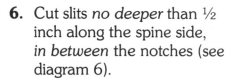

6

7. Open the folds so that there are an equal number of folds on each side. At one end, staple through all layers as shown in diagram 7.

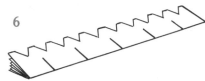

7

8. Open up the unstapled end to form the fish's mouth (see diagram 8).

8

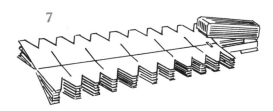

9. Tape about *every other hill fold* closed at the mouth end (see diagram 9).

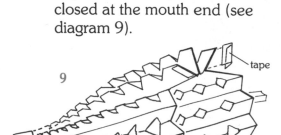

9

tape

10. Cut out the mouth part and tape in place as shown in diagram 10. (Make sure the tail end is vertical before you tape the mouth in place.)

10

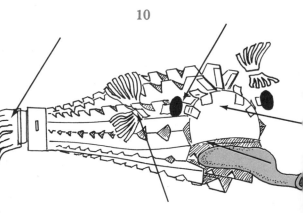

11. Cut out the tail, fins, and eyes and tape in place as shown.

12. Put a balloon inside the fish so that the opening sticks out of the fish's mouth. Blow up the balloon and watch the fish puff up. When you let the air out, the fish will deflate to its original shape.

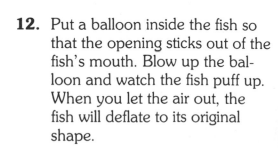

Branching Out

- Puffing up is one way animals defend themselves. Do some research to find out more about other animals that puff themselves up for self-defense: hognose snake, swallowtail caterpillar, horned lizard, American toad, chuckwalla.
- See *NatureScope—Diving into Oceans* for more activities about marine fish and other sea creatures.

Ellen Lambeth

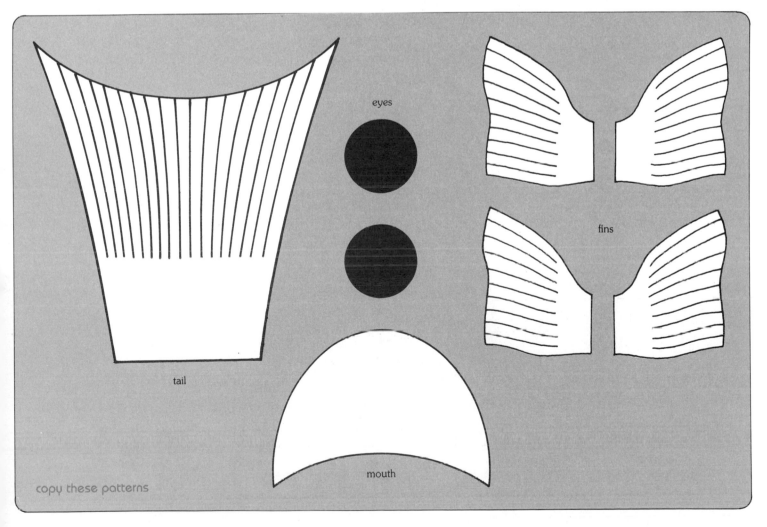

tail

eyes

fins

mouth

copy these patterns

Pine Cone Birds

Turn pine cones into colorful birds.

Ages:
Advanced

Materials for one bird:
- *pine cones of differ- ent sizes*
- *filbert (hazelnut) or other nut*
- *flexible wire (about 22 gauge) or long pipe cleaner*
- *construction paper*
- *tacky glue*
- *clay*
- *scissors*
- *paints (acrylics work best) and paintbrush*
- *pictures of birds*

1. Look at some pictures of birds and select a bird to use as a model. Jays, chickadees, titmice, cardinals, bobwhites, finches, and owls make good models.

2. Choose a small pine cone (about 3 inches long) that matches the shape of the bird's body. Cones that are fully opened work best.

3. Wrap about a foot of wire (or a long pipe cleaner) tightly around the middle of the pine cone, leaving about 3 inches free on each end. Shape the two ends into feet. Make sure the feet are

close to the body and that they face forward, toward the wider end of the cone (see diagram).

4. Put a dot of tacky glue where the head should be and then put a small bit of clay over the glue. Put another dot of glue on the clay and attach the rounded end of a filbert (see diagram).

glue

5. To make wings, break off two scales from a large pine cone. Use scissors to trim the wings into shape and then glue them in place.

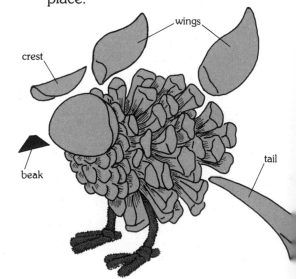

crest

wings

beak

tail

Fun Facts

- Pine trees produce two kinds of cones: tiny male cones, which bear pollen, and the more familiar female cones, which bear seeds.

- Jays, nuthatches, chipmunks, mice, and other animals eat the seeds that grow on the under- sides of a pine cone's scales.

- The sugar pine of the western United States produces some of the largest cones. These cones get to be nearly 2 feet long!

- Hemlocks produce some of the smallest female cones. These tiny cones are only about ½ inch long.

chipmunk

6. To make the bird's tail, break off a very large pine scale. Glue it in place so that it helps the bird stand up. (The feet and tail should act as a tripod to hold the bird up.)

7. To make a beak, cut out a small construction paper triangle. Fold it in half and glue it to the end of the nut. To make a crest for a jay, titmouse, or cardinal, cut out a small circle from construction paper. Fold the circle in half and glue it on top of the nut. Let the glue dry completely.

8. Paint the bird, making sure that you get the paint down inside the cone scales as far as possible. Also paint on eyes, markings, and other features.

Branching Out

● Pine cones make great bird feeders. Just tie a piece of yarn or string around a cone and fill the spaces between its scales with a mixture of peanut butter, melted suet, and birdseed. Then tie the feeder in a place where you can watch the birds feast!

Prairie Dog

Mold a prairie dog and lead it through a maze of tunnels.

Ages:
Primary

Materials for one prairie dog and maze:
- *copy of pages 38 and 39*
- *crayons or markers*
- *two small, strong magnets*
- *18 × 24-inch piece of oaktag or poster-board*
- *tape*
- *paint and paintbrush*
- *wax paper*
- *measuring cup*
- *cornstarch*
- *baking soda*
- *water*
- *saucepan and spoon*
- *plate*
- *stove*
- *damp cloth*
- *plastic bag*
- *refrigerator*

1. Mold a simple inch-long prairie dog out of craft dough (see recipe at right). Be sure not to use too much dough or your prairie dog will be too heavy for the magnet to move.

2. Push a magnet into the *flat* bottom of the prairie dog (see diagram). Make sure that the bottom of the magnet isn't covered by the dough. Set the prairie dog on wax paper and let dry overnight.

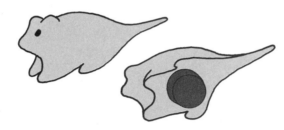

3. When the craft-dough prairie dog is completely dry and hardened, paint it and let dry.

4. Color the two halves of the maze and tape them together. Tape the maze onto an 18 × 24-inch piece of oaktag or posterboard.

5. Place the magnetic prairie dog near the burrow opening on the maze and hold another magnet underneath the maze board. Make the prairie dog run through the tunnels of its burrow by moving the magnet underneath. See the information under "Fun Facts" to learn how prairie dogs use each of the chambers in their burrows.

Craft Dough Recipe

This recipe will make enough dough for at least five prairie dogs:

- ½ cup baking soda
- ¼ cup cornstarch
- ¼ cup plus 3 T cold water

Mix all of the ingredients in a medium-sized saucepan and cook over medium heat, stirring constantly. Cook until the mixture is the consistency of mashed potatoes (about 10 minutes). Remove from heat, turn out onto a plate, and cover with a damp cloth. Let the dough cool and then knead it into a smooth ball. Store the dough in a tightly sealed plastic bag and refrigerate until you're ready to use it.

Branching Out

- Make a list of animals that have homes with tunnels and special chambers. Some examples are honey bees, termites, badgers, moles, and ants.
- To trace a path through an ant colony, try "An Ant's A-mazing World" on page 42 of *NatureScope—Incredible Insects.*
- Read a book about prairie dogs to find out more about these North American rodents.
- Use the craft dough to make other types of animals, and create your own mazes.

Puzzler

Fun Facts

- Early American settlers gave the prairie dog its name because they thought the rodent's alarm call sounded like a dog's bark.

- Most prairie dog burrows contain a nursery chamber, a grass-lined sleeping chamber, a toilet room, a listening post near the burrow's entrance, and a chamber close to the surface that usually doesn't flood, even during heavy rains.

- Most prairie dogs live together in "towns." Some of these towns may cover more than 150 acres!

prairie dogs

Make oatmeal-container animals that can "talk."

Ages:
Intermediate

Materials:
- **oatmeal container**
- **construction paper**
- **tape**
- **glue**
- **sharp scissors**
- **marker**

To make a lion:
- **2-foot piece of nylon or jute twine**
- **pencil**

To make a frog:
- **rubber band**

1. Remove the lid from an oatmeal container and cover both the container and the top of the lid with construction paper.

2. To make the lion's mane, cut out a strip of construction paper that's 2 inches wide and about 13 inches long. Glue the strip around the lid. Cut slits about ⅛ inch apart all the way around the strip to make a fringe (see diagram). Bend the fringe outward.

3. Cut out paper eyes, ears, whiskers, and a nose, and glue them onto the lid. Draw in a mouth and any other features.

4. Tape the lid to the oatmeal container so that the face hangs on the side of the container as shown in the diagram.

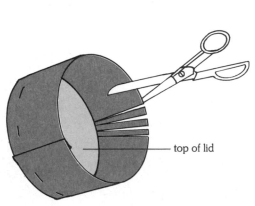

top of lid

Fun Facts

- Lions live in groups called **prides.**

- Lions communicate through growls, grunts, and purrs, as well as roars.

- A lion's roar can be heard up to 5 miles away. To strange lions it is a warning to keep away. To fellow pride members it means, "I'm over here."

male and female African lion

and...

5. Cut out paper feet and a tail and glue them to the bottom of the container.

6. Tie a large knot at one end of a 2-foot piece of twine. Then use a pencil to poke a small hole in the bottom of the container. Reach inside the container and thread the unknotted end of the twine through the hole. (The knot should keep the twine from pulling all the way through the hole.) Then tie a knot at the other end of the twine to keep it from unraveling.

7. To make the lion roar, hold the twine between your thumb and first finger and run your nail down the twine.

Lion craft by Peter Hamilton Kent. Adapted from *Ranger Rick*, March 1979.

Plunky Green Frog

1. Remove the lid from an oatmeal container and cover both the container and the lid with green construction paper.

2. Use sharp scissors to cut a tab near the edge of each side of the lid and then bend the tabs up (see diagram). Put the lid on the container.

3. Cut a frog face and eyes out of construction paper and glue the eyes to the face. Draw in a mouth and nostrils, then glue the finished face to the side of the container.

4. Cut frog feet out of construction paper and glue them to the bottom of the container. Also cut out an egg-shaped piece of white construction paper and glue it below the face to make the frog's belly.

5. To make the green frog call, stretch a rubber band around the tabs on the lid and plunk it with your finger.

Fun Facts

- Male frogs call to attract a mate. Each species has its own type of call, and females respond only to calls from males of their own species.

- The call of a green frog sounds like the twang of a loose banjo string.

- Male frogs sometimes call together in small groups, creating mating **choruses.** These loud frog choruses may help attract females to a mating area.

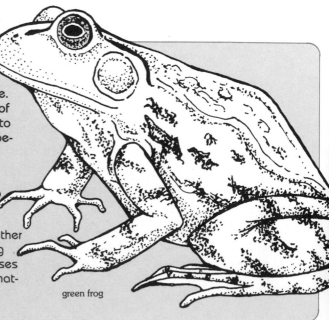

green frog

Branching Out

- Trills, whistles, and barks are some of the many sounds that frogs make. Take a night hike to listen to frog calls. See "Call of the Wild" on page 26 of *Nature-Scope—Let's Hear It for Herps!* for some frog-calling and frog-watching tips.

- Vocalization is just one of the ways animals communicate. Try "Face It!" on page 7 of *Nature-Scope—Amazing Mammals II* to find out how some primates (people and chimpanzees) use facial expressions to communicate.

Wacky Beastie

Make mix-and-match animal blocks.

Ages:
Primary

Materials for one set of blocks:
- **copy of patterns on pages 46 and 47**
- **crayons or markers**
- **glue**
- **oaktag or poster-board**
- **scissors**
- **tape**

1. Color the pictures on the pattern pages. (Find the top and bottom of each animal so you can make them the same color.)

2. Spread a *thin* film of glue over the entire back of each pattern and place the pattern on a piece of oaktag or posterboard. Let dry, then cut out the patterns along the solid lines.

3. Form the cut-outs into cubes by folding along each dashed line. Then tape the tab next to the frog square underneath the raccoon

square. Fold up the two sides, insert the tabs, and tape them closed.

4. Stack the blocks to make crazy, mixed-up animals or match the tops and bottoms to form "real" creatures.

Branching Out

- Use the blocks to compare the six different animals on the blocks. Discuss how the creatures are different and how they're the same.
- Make up names for the mixed-up animals you create. First, split the real names in two. (rac-coon, ea-gle, octo-pus, gold-fish, bull-frog, alli-gator) Then put them back together in mixed-up ways. For example, the alligator head

Fun Facts

- Many mythical creatures—such as sphinxes, centaurs, and mermaids—are part human and part animal.

- The mule—a cross between a donkey and a horse—is a hybrid that's been around for thousands of years.

- Asian farmers breed yaks with cows to produce "yakows," which are bigger and stronger and produce more milk than their parents.

yakow

Blocks

with the octopus body could be called an "allipus." Or the octopus head on the alligator's body could become an "octogator." Make up stories about where each "mixed-up" creature lives, what it eats, what sounds it makes, and so on.

- Discuss some real mixed-up animals called *hybrids*—the offspring of animals that don't normally interbreed. (For more information about hybrids, see "Half and Half" in *Ranger Rick*, Sept. 1987, pp. 32–36.)

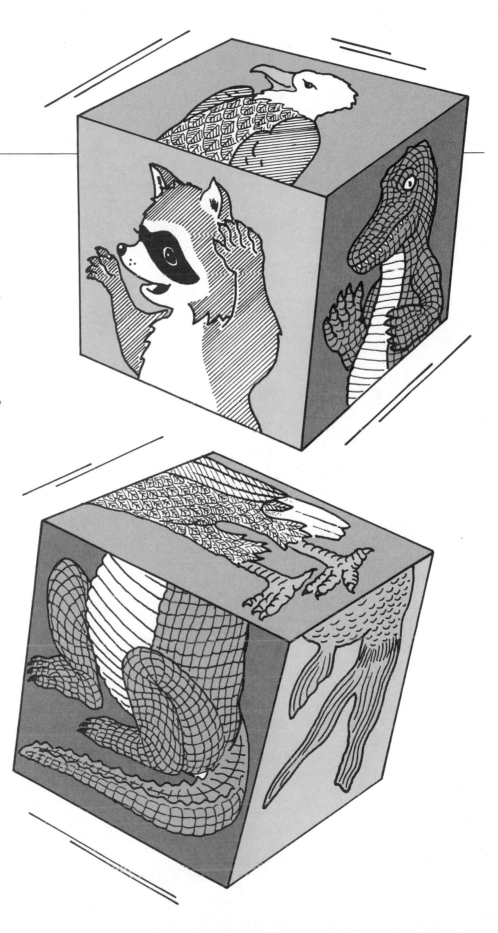

copy this pattern

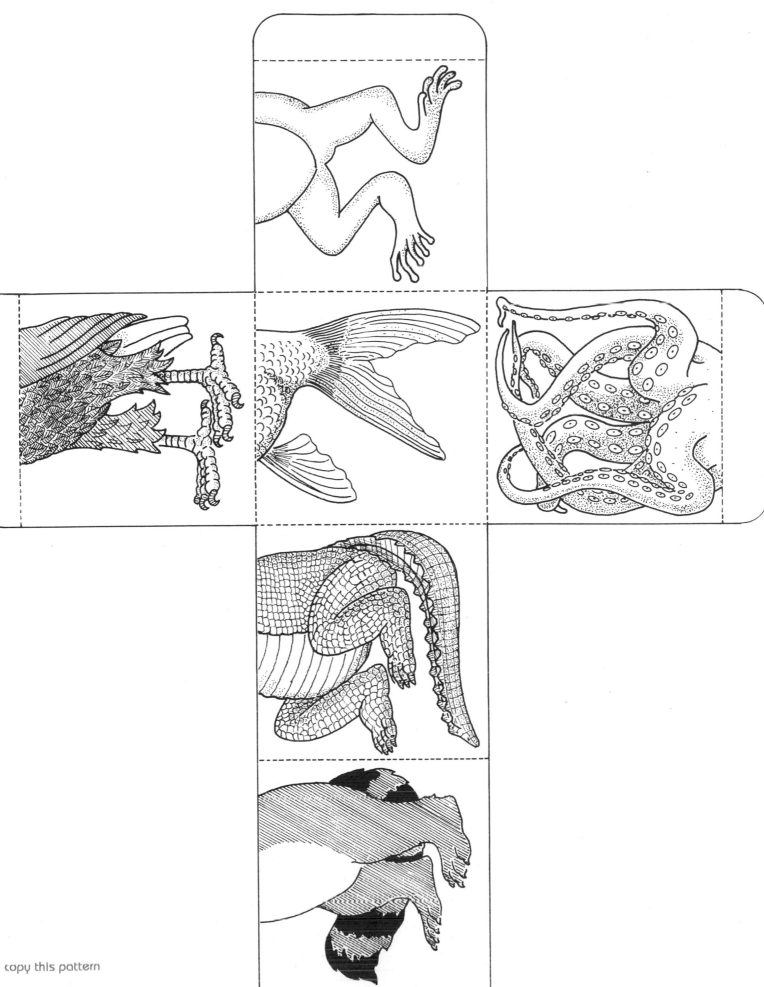

copy this pattern

47

Weave a Fish

Make a patterned fish by weaving paper "scales" across its body.

Ages:
Primary and Intermediate

Materials for one fish:
- **construction paper**
- **scissors**
- **glue or tape**
- **ruler**
- **ribbon (optional)**

1. Draw a fish shape on a piece of construction paper and cut it out.

2. Fold the fish shape in half lengthwise and cut straight or wavy slits across the middle of the body (see diagram). The slits should be about ½ to 1 inch apart, depending on the size of the fish. (Be careful not to cut too close to the edges.) Unfold the fish and set aside.

3. Cut strips from a different-colored sheet of construction paper or from ribbon. The strips should be about ½ to 1 inch wide and long enough to weave through all the slits you cut.

4. Weave "scales" into your fish with the strips, forming a checkerboard pattern in the fish's body. Once the strips are in place, trim off any excess paper or ribbon and glue or tape the ends down.

5. Cut out construction paper eyes and glue them onto both sides of the fish. Cut fringes in the fish's fins and tail.

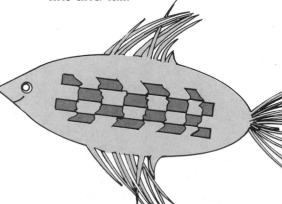

Fun Facts

- Most fish are protected by tough, overlapping scales. But some fish, such as lampreys and freshwater catfish, have no scales at all.

- Not all scaly fish have "regular" scales. For example, pinecone fish have spiny scales, and seahorses are covered with armorlike plates.

- The "stinger" on a stingray's tail is a modified scale.

- Scientists can often estimate the age of a fish by counting growth rings on its scales.

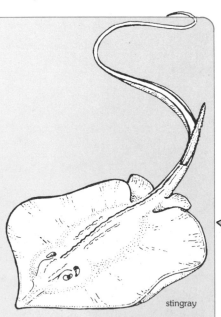

stingray

Branching Out

- Make a fish mobile out of several woven fish. Or make a hanging model of a jellyfish and attach fish to its tentacles. (Certain types of small fish seek refuge from predators among the poisonous tentacles of certain types of jellyfish. The smaller fish seem to be immune to the jellyfish's poison.) To make the model, tape pieces of ribbon, some of them curled, to a paper plate to represent the jellyfish's tentacles. Then attach a few fish to the ten-

tacles. (See "Jazzy Jellyfish" on page 66 of *NatureScope—Diving into Oceans* for more complete instructions on how to make a jellyfish.)
- Make other kinds of scaly animals. For example, you can weave scales into paper snakes, lizards, or butterflies. (Butterfly wings are covered with thousands of tiny scales.)
- See *NatureScope—Diving into Oceans* for more activities about marine fish and other sea creatures.

Wild Masks

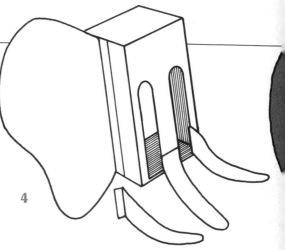

Make animal masks out of shoeboxes.

Elephant Mask

Ages:
Intermediate

Materials:
- **shoebox**
- **ruler**
- **pencil**
- **paper punch**
- **transparent tape**
- **sharp scissors**
- **paint and paintbrush**
- **string or ribbon**

To make an elephant:
- **oaktag or poster-board**
- **glue**

To make a pelican:
- **32-inch piece of flexible wire (about 22 gauge)**
- **large piece of tissue paper**
- **two paper fasteners**
- **masking tape**

1. Mark two long, narrow strips on the bottom of a shoebox, as shown. The strips should be about 1½ inches wide and 1½ inches apart. Also, the rounded top of each strip should be about 3½ inches from the end of the box. Cut out the two strips (see diagram 1).

2. Tape one of the cut-out eye strips to the center strip, rounded end down, to form a trunk (see diagram 2).

3. Cut two ears, each with a ½-inch tab along the straight edge, out of oaktag or poster-board (see diagram 3). Fold the tabs and tape or glue them onto the sides of the box as shown in diagram 4.

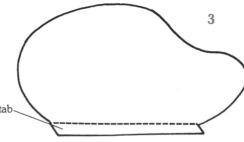

4. If you wish, cut two tusks out of oaktag or posterboard and tape them to the sides of the box at the bottom edges (see diagram 4).

5. Paint the elephant mask and let dry. Then paint on wrinkles and other features and let dry.

6. Punch a hole in each side of the box, about a third of the way down. Attach a piece of string or ribbon to each hole as shown in diagram 5.

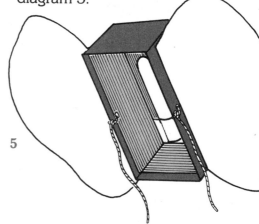

7. Put the mask on, letting the top of the box rest on your head. Have someone tie the string or ribbon around the back of your head.

Fun Facts

- Many people in different parts of the world wear animal masks in special ceremonies. They believe that the masks help them communicate with the spirits of animals that are important to them.

- The Mandan Indians of North America depended on the buffalo for food, clothing, and shelter. These Native Americans wore buffalo masks during a dance to show their appreciation for the animal. They also believed it would increase their chances for a successful hunt.

- The Northwest Coast Indians created intricate "transformation masks" that were actually two masks in one. The outer part of the mask looked like a bird, such as a raven or eagle. The bird's beak could be pulled open by strings to reveal the second mask inside—that of a human face.

Pelican Mask

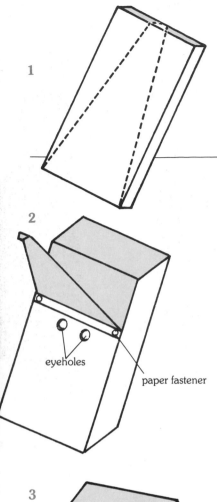

1

2

eyeholes

paper fastener

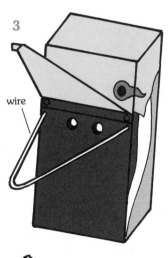

3

wire

4

masking tape

1. Put a shoebox over your face, resting one end on top of your head. Make marks where the eyeholes should be. After removing the box, use sharp scissors to poke a hole through each mark. Then enlarge the holes just enough so you can see out of them.

2. Cut a triangle out of a shoebox lid to form the top of the pelican's beak (see diagram 1). *Note:* When you cut out the triangle, don't cut off the rim on either end of the lid. The rim will form a hinge at the base of the beak and a hook at the tip of the beak.

3. Using sharp scissors, poke a hole on each side of the beak's hinge. Put paper fasteners through the holes and then poke them through the bottom of the shoebox so that the hinge is right above the eyeholes (see diagram 2). Secure the fasteners inside the box.

4. Paint the pelican and let dry. Be sure to paint the pelican's eyes near the sides of the shoebox, above the beak.

5. Bend a 32-inch piece of wire into a "V." Poke the ends through the shoebox, about 1½ inches below the beak and near the sides of the box (see diagram 3). Push the wire ends through the holes until about 4 inches of wire come

through the inside of the box on each side. Bend the ends of the wires down and tape them in place as shown. *Safety Note:* Be sure to cover the wire ends completely with masking tape so they can't scratch you (see diagram 4).

5

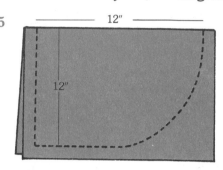

12"

12"

6. Fold a large piece of tissue paper in half and cut out a shape that will make a half circle when you open it (see diagram 5). The shape should be about 12 inches wide and about 12 inches long.

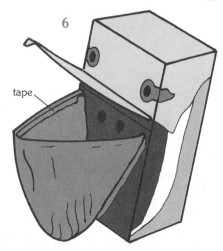

6

tape

7. To form the pelican's pouch, fold the straight edge of the tissue paper over the wire and tape in place with transparent tape.

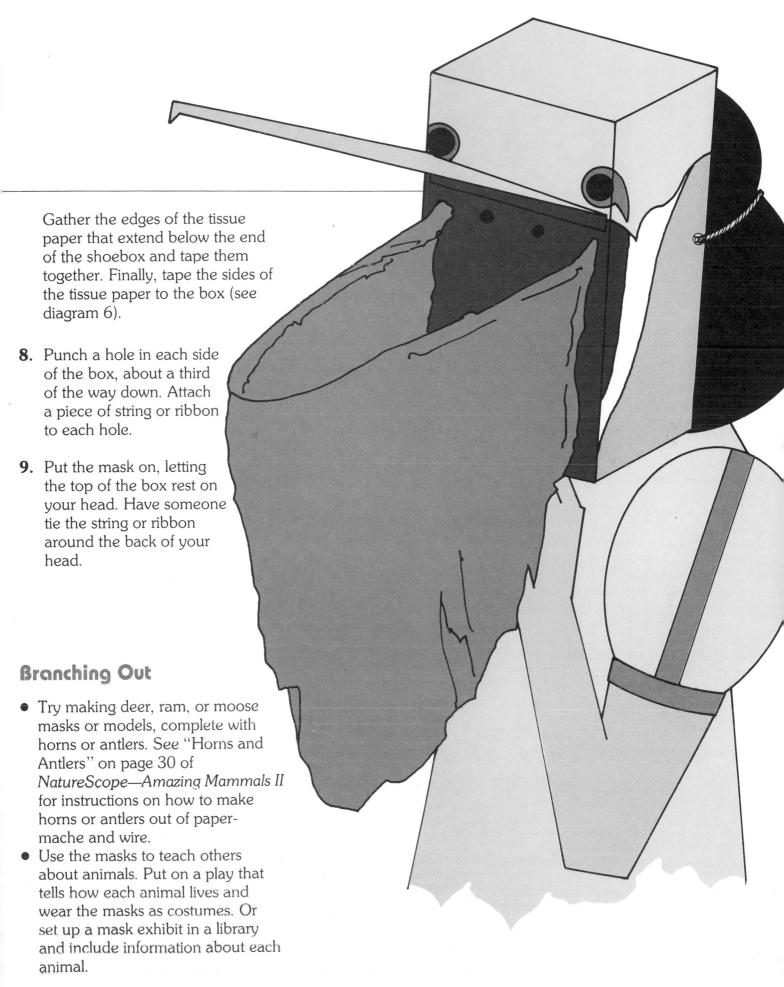

Gather the edges of the tissue paper that extend below the end of the shoebox and tape them together. Finally, tape the sides of the tissue paper to the box (see diagram 6).

8. Punch a hole in each side of the box, about a third of the way down. Attach a piece of string or ribbon to each hole.

9. Put the mask on, letting the top of the box rest on your head. Have someone tie the string or ribbon around the back of your head.

Branching Out

- Try making deer, ram, or moose masks or models, complete with horns or antlers. See "Horns and Antlers" on page 30 of *NatureScope—Amazing Mammals II* for instructions on how to make horns or antlers out of paper-mache and wire.
- Use the masks to teach others about animals. Put on a play that tells how each animal lives and wear the masks as costumes. Or set up a mask exhibit in a library and include information about each animal.

Wind Flower

Make a pinwheel flower.

Ages:
Primary and Intermediate

Materials for one pinwheel:
- *pictures of flowers with four petals*
- *colored paper*
- *pencil with eraser*
- *round-headed straight pin*
- *glue*
- *scissors*
- *ruler*
- *markers*

1. Look at some pictures of flowers that have four petals (evening primroses, bluets, dogwoods, poppies, and so on) and choose one for a model.

2. Cut a piece of colored paper into a square. Each side of the square should be 6–9 inches long.

3. Fold the square in half diagonally and crease it. Unfold it and then make another diagonal fold so that the two folds form an "X." Mark the center of the X to make it easier to see later.

4. Cut along the fold lines from each corner to about 1½ inches from the center. Be careful not to cut too close to the center or the pinwheel won't spin.

5. Cut out a paper center for the flower. Depending on the type of flower you're making, the center can be a simple circle or it can be more elaborate, with fringes or other details.

6. Push a straight pin through the front of the flower center. Then curl every other point of the cut square in toward the center and push the pin through each one in turn, about ¼ inch from the tip (see diagram). Finally push the pin through the center of the square where you marked the X.

7. Push the pin into the side of the eraser on a pencil. (Push it until the point *almost* comes

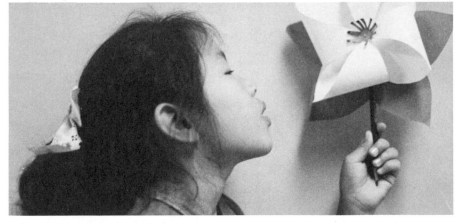

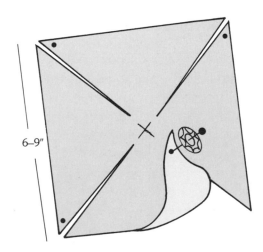

6–9"

Fun Facts

- Wind pollinates many plants and often picks up and carries pollen great distances—sometimes hundreds of miles from its source.

- The seeds of dandelions, milkweeds, and many other plants have silky hairs that catch the wind and parachute the seeds into new areas.

- A wind-pollinated plant produces pollen grains by the millions so that at least some of them will be blown onto another flower of the same type.

through the opposite side, but make sure it doesn't come all the way through.)

8. Trim the petals to match the shape of the flower you're making. Add any features to the petals or to the flower's center.

9. Cut out paper leaves and glue them to the pencil, behind the flower. (Make sure you don't get glue on the flower or it won't spin later.) Let the glue dry completely.

10. Make the wind flower spin by blowing into the paper petals or by swirling it through the air.

Branching Out

● To find out how different animals and plants "use" the wind, see "The Ways of the Wind" on page 18 of *NatureScope—Wild about Weather.*

● Take the wind flower outside on a breezy day and use it to find out which way the wind is blowing. (To record wind direction and speed, try "Make a Wind Sock" on page 60 of *NatureScope—Wild about Weather.*)

● Name several things that catch the wind, such as windmills, weathervanes, kites, sails, wind socks, and so on.

1998 Update

Table of Contents

Gulping Alligator

Make an alligator that eats and wiggles its tail.

Ages:
**Primary,
Intermediate**

Materials for one alligator:
- **copy of patterns on page 58**
- **green construction paper**
- **toilet paper roll cylinder**
- **ruler**
- **scissors**
- **white glue**
- **paper punch**
- **water-base markers**
- **metal paper fastener**
- **white paper napkin**

1. Use the patterns to trace a tail and four legs onto green construction paper. Cut them out and set them aside.

2. To make the alligator body, use the ruler to draw a $4\frac{1}{2} \times 6$ inch ($11\frac{1}{2} \times 15$ centimeters) rectangle on the green paper. Cut it out. Spread glue on it. Wrap it around the toilet paper roll cylinder, covering the cylinder completely.

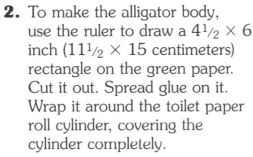

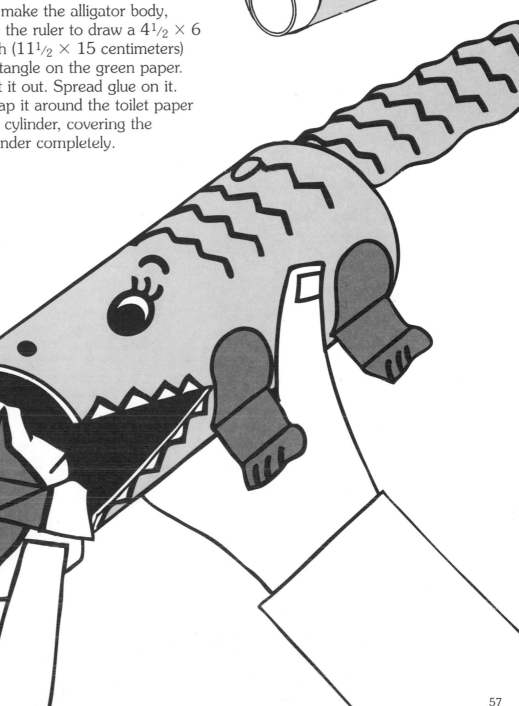

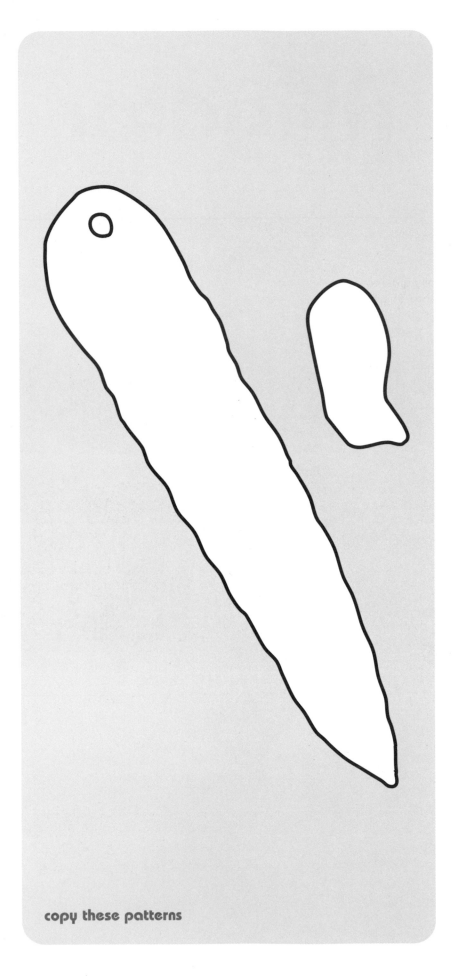

3. Cut a V shape on both sides of one end of the cylinder to make a mouth for the alligator. Use markers to draw eyes, eyebrows, and nostrils. Draw wavy lines for skin and zigzag lines for teeth.

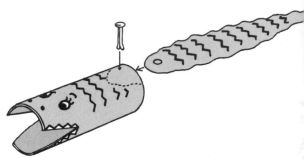

4. Use a paper punch to make a hole in the top of the alligator's back and another hole in the tail. Fasten the tail to the body with a metal paper fastener. The tail can wiggle back and forth.

5. Glue the legs to the sides of the body.

6. Use markers to draw pictures of alligator food on the paper napkin. Wad up the napkin and "feed" it to the alligator by pushing it into its mouth.

copy these patterns

Fun Facts

- In the United States, alligators live in the Southeast along the edges of lakes, swamps, and rivers. They dig burrows for hiding in case of danger. Alligators hibernate in the burrows during cold weather.

- Alligators have broader snouts than crocodiles.

- Alligators usually grow to be 6 to 12 feet (2 to 3½ meters) long.

- Alligators usually eat fish, birds, and small animals.

- Alligators make a hissing sound. Male alligators can roar loudly.

- A female alligator lays 20 to 70 eggs, buries them in a mud nest, and then guards them until the babies safely hatch.

Branching Out

- Find out more about an alligator's habitat. Draw a picture of a place an alligator might like to live. Roll up the picture and insert it in your Gulping Alligator. Its body is a good paper holder.

- So many alligators were killed in the United States that they had to be protected from hunters. Can you discover why people hunted alligators?

Dancing Daddy

Make a daddy long-legs using a gum ball, which is the seed pod of a sweet gum tree, or a foam craft ball.

Ages:
*Primary,
Intermediate,
Advanced*

Materials for one daddy longlegs:
- *A gum ball with stem from a sweet gum tree or a foam craft ball 2 inches (5 centimeters) in diameter*
- *8 brown or black pipe cleaners*
- *scissors*
- *white glue*
- *scrap paper or jar lid*
- *paper punch*
- *yarn or string*

1. Cut the pipe cleaners into 5-inch (13-centimeter) lengths.

2. Pour a small amount of glue onto scrap paper or into an old jar lid.

3. Dip the end of each pipe cleaner in the glue, and insert it into the gum ball or foam craft ball. Insert four legs on one side and four legs on the other side. If you are using a gum ball, be sure the stem is at the top of your daddy longlegs.

4. After the glue dries, bend each leg up at the base of the body. Then bend each leg down in the middle. Bend a tiny foot on the end of each leg.

5. Glue on two eyes made of paper punch circles.

6. Tie string or yarn onto the gum ball stem. If you are using a foam ball, staple a string to the top.

7. Jiggle the string and watch your daddy longlegs dance!

Fun Facts

- The daddy longlegs is also called the harvestman. Its name comes from its long legs, which reminded people of harvesters' scythes.

- The daddy longlegs is a cousin of the spider. It has eight legs, like a spider, but only two eyes.

- The daddy longlegs is not poisonous. It eats dead insects and old wood and leaves. If it is frightened, it gives off a liquid that makes it smell and taste bad.

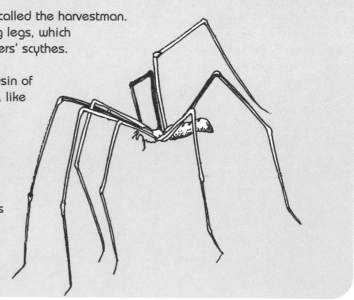

Longlegs

Branching Out

- At one time, farm children who had to find the cows for milking at the end of the day sometimes asked a daddy longlegs to tell them where the cows were. They believed that the daddy longlegs would point its long front legs in the correct direction! This belief is called a myth. What other myths can you find?

- Some people think that daddy longlegs are poisonous, but they are not. This belief is called a misconception. People also used to think that strawberries were poisonous. How do you think misconceptions originate? Can you discover other popular misconceptions?

- Daddy longlegs are often mistaken for spiders. All spiders have certain features that daddy longlegs do not have. Can you discover some of the things that distinguish spiders from daddy longlegs?

Egg-Laying

Make a bald eagle that lays an egg and snuggles an eaglet under her wing.

Ages:
Primary, Intermediate

Materials for one bald eagle:
- **copy of patterns on pages 64–65.**
- **white poster board**
- **yellow and black construction paper**
- **scissors**
- **white glue**
- **crayons**
- **black marker**
- **paper punch**
- **cotton ball**
- **brown powdered tempera paint**
- **plastic sandwich bag**
- **a safety razor blade for an adult to use**

1. Use the patterns to trace the eagle body, egg, feet, and wing onto poster board. Cut them out.

2. Use a black marker to draw the eagle's face as shown. Color the body brown with a white head, neck, and tail. Color the beak and feet yellow. Glue on a yellow construction paper eye made with a paper punch. Glue on the feet.

3. An adult should use the razor to make two slits, 1 inch (2.5 centimeters) long each, in the eagle body as the pattern shows.

4. Glue Point A on the wing to Point A on the body.

5. To make an eaglet, color the cotton ball brown with powered tempera paint. To do this, put the cotton ball in a plastic sandwich bag, sift in a little paint, and shake.

6. Glue the cotton ball eaglet below the body slit. Add two black construction paper eyes made with the paper punch. Glue a yellow beak below the eyes. Glue the eaglet to Point B under the wing.

Fun Facts

- The bald eagle has been the national bird of the United States since 1782. It is the only eagle that lives just in North America.

- Eagles are monogamous. This means that they keep the same mate throughout their life.

- Eagles build large nests of sticks and twigs in rocky crevices and tall trees. They often use the same nest over and over, repairing it each year.

- Eagles like to eat fish. They prefer to nest by rivers and large lakes.

Bald Eagle

7. Insert Tab C of the egg through slit C, from back to front, and then through slit D, from front to back.

8. Pull Tab C so that the egg is hidden behind the eagle. Push the tab so the eagle can lay the egg.

Branching Out

- The bald eagle can grow up to 40 inches (1 meter) long. It has a dark brown body, white head and tail, and yellow beak, eyes, and feet. Use a yardstick and bulletin board paper to draw a life-size model of our national bird.

- Bald eagles need no protection except from humans. They have been protected since 1940 under the National Emblem Act. This means that no one is allowed to kill them. Find out about other protected birds.

- Chemicals used in farming threaten the bald eagle. Can you discover why? Use these key words to help your research: DDT, pest control.

- From 1917 until 1940, Alaska paid bounty hunters to kill bald eagles. It was thought that eagles scared salmon away from fishing nets. This killing of bald eagles is one of the reasons that they are endangered. What else can you find out about present-day bald eagles?

copy this pattern

64

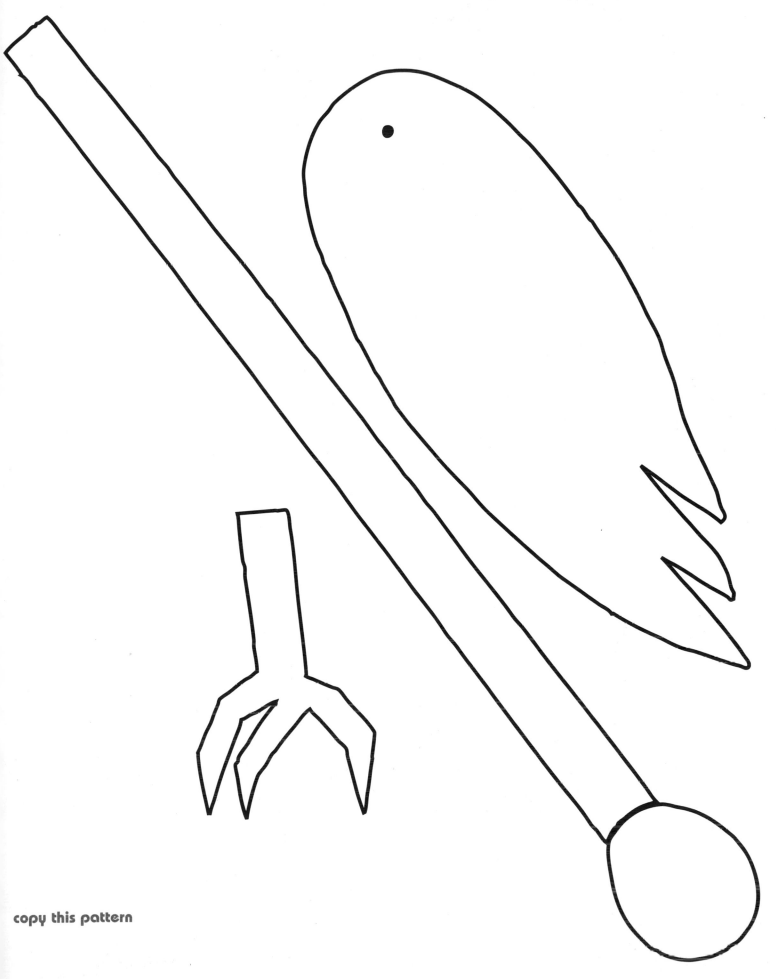

copy this pattern

Wild Turkey

You can make a turkey that really gobbles by combining a plastic cup, a string, and a piece of wet sponge.

Ages:
Primary, Intermediate, Advanced

Materials for one wild turkey:
- copy of patterns on page 68
- 16-ounce (1/2-liter) yellow disposable plastic drinking cup
- black permanent marker with a narrow tip
- red, orange, and brown construction paper
- household cement (such as Duco)
- ruler
- scissors
- 24-inch-long (61-centimeter-long) piece of embroidery thread
- household sponge cut into a 2-inch (5-centimeter) square
- water
- paper clip

1. Ask an adult to poke a small hole in the middle of the cup's bottom.

2. Turn the cup upside down. Draw two eyes on the cup with the black marker.

3. Use the patterns to trace a red wattle, orange beak, and brown wings and tail on construction paper. Cut them out and glue them onto the cup with household cement. Let the glue dry.

Fun Facts

- Turkeys are native to North America. They were named by English settlers who thought they resembled the guinea hen from Islamic (or Turkish) lands.

- Wild turkeys are dark-colored with iridescent bronze and green feathers. A male turkey is called a tom, a female is a hen, and baby turkeys are called poults.

- Although wild turkeys usually run away when frightened, they can also fly 1/4 mile (402 meters) at a time.

- Turkeys eat insects, seeds, and an occasional frog or lizard.

- The turkey hen lays 8 to 15 brownish spotted eggs in a hollow in the ground. She keeps them warm until the poults hatch 28 days later.

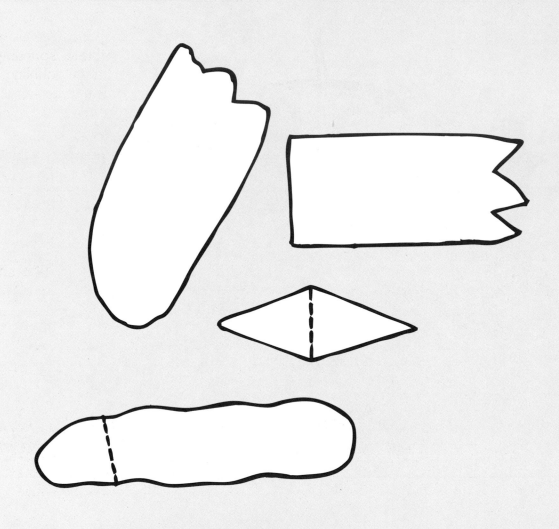

copy this pattern

4. Use a ruler and scissors to measure and cut a 24-inch-long (61-centimeter-long) piece of embroidery thread. Also measure and cut a 2-inch (5-centimeter) square of household sponge. Dip the sponge in water and then squeeze it to remove as much water as possible.

5. Tie one end of the thread very tightly around the middle of the damp sponge. Put the other end of the thread inside the cup, and poke it through the hole.

6. Tie it to a paper clip so that the sponge hangs suspended below the upside-down cup.

7. To make the turkey gobble, grasp the top of the string with the damp sponge, and pull down with a quick, steady motion. The wet sponge causes the string to vibrate, sounding like a turkey gobbling. The cup acts as an amplifier to make the vibrations louder.

Branching Out

- Turkeys have been domesticated for hundreds of years. What can you find out about turkey farming methods?

- When turkey poults hatch, they imprint to the turkey hen. Imprinting is important for the survival of the babies. Find out more about this interesting instinct by using your library or media center.

- Imprinting is an instinct. What other instincts do some animals have?

Dimetrodon

Make a dimetrodon family with these instructions for parent and baby.

Ages:
*Primary,
Intermediate,
Advanced*

Materials for one dimetrodon parent and one baby:
- copy of patterns on pages 72–73.
- construction paper
- paper towel roll cylinder (parent)
- toilet paper roll cylinder (baby)
- ruler
- scissors
- white glue
- water-base markers
- poster paper

Dimetrodon Parent:

1. Trace and cut out the patterns. To make the fin, fold a sheet of construction paper in half. Lay the top of the pattern on the fold. Trace and cut out. Outline the fin with a black marker. Draw spines on it. To make the tail, fold a 3 × 7 inch (7½ × 18 centimeter) piece of paper in half lengthwise. Lay the top of the pattern on the fold. Trace and cut out. Draw lines on the tail. To make legs, trace two legs onto poster paper. Cut them out. Color them. Draw feet and claws with a marker. Set these aside.

2. To make the dimetrodon body, cut a 9 × 11 inch (23 × 28 centimeter) rectangle from construction paper. Spread glue on it. Wrap it around the paper towel roll cylinder to cover.

3. Spread glue along the inside bottom edges of the fin. Glue the fin on each side of the body.

4. Put glue on the wide end of the tail. Glue the tail inside the cylinder body.

5. Cut a V shape on both sides of one end of the cylinder to make a mouth for the dimetrodon. Use markers to draw eyes, eyebrows, and nostrils.

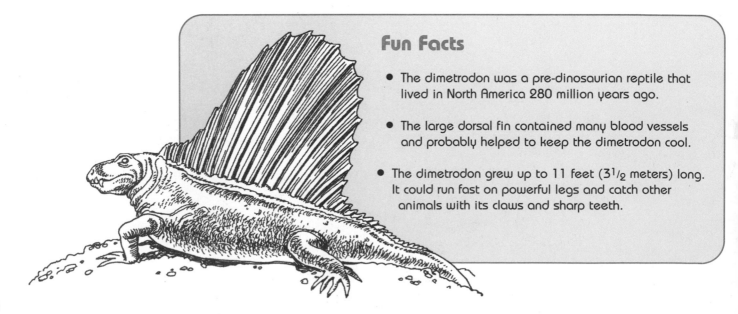

Fun Facts

- The dimetrodon was a pre-dinosaurian reptile that lived in North America 280 million years ago.

- The large dorsal fin contained many blood vessels and probably helped to keep the dimetrodon cool.

- The dimetrodon grew up to 11 feet (3½ meters) long. It could run fast on powerful legs and catch other animals with its claws and sharp teeth.

Parent and Baby

6. Fold the legs on the dotted lines. Put glue on the insides of the rounded edges and attach the legs to the body. Set the dimetrodon upright while you glue its legs on so that it will stand straight. Then lay it on its side to dry.

Dimetrodon Baby:

1. Use a toilet paper roll cylinder for the body. Draw a $4\frac{1}{2} \times 6$ inches (10×15 centimeter) rectangle on construction paper. Cut it out. Spread glue on it. Wrap it around the toilet-paper roll cylinder, covering the cylinder completely.

2. Follow the directions for the parent but use the smaller patterns.

Branching Out

- We know about animals like the dimetrodon because of fossil remains. What other information can you discover about fossils?

- People who study forms of life that existed long ago, in different geological periods, are called paleontologists. Find out how you might spend a day as a real paleontologist.

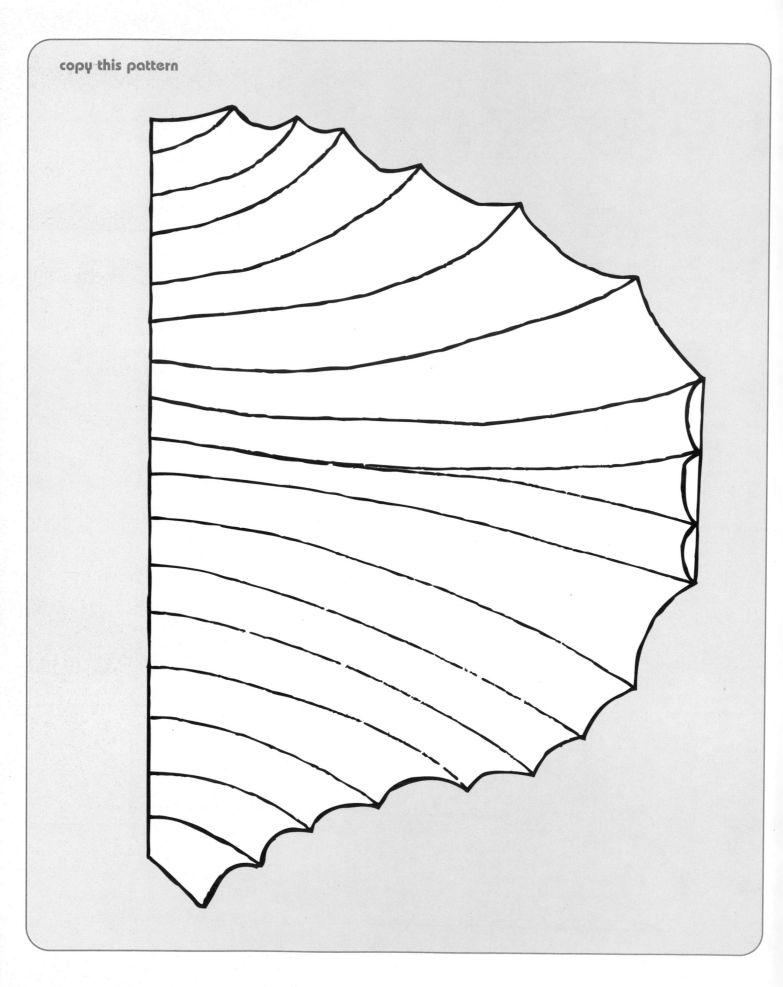

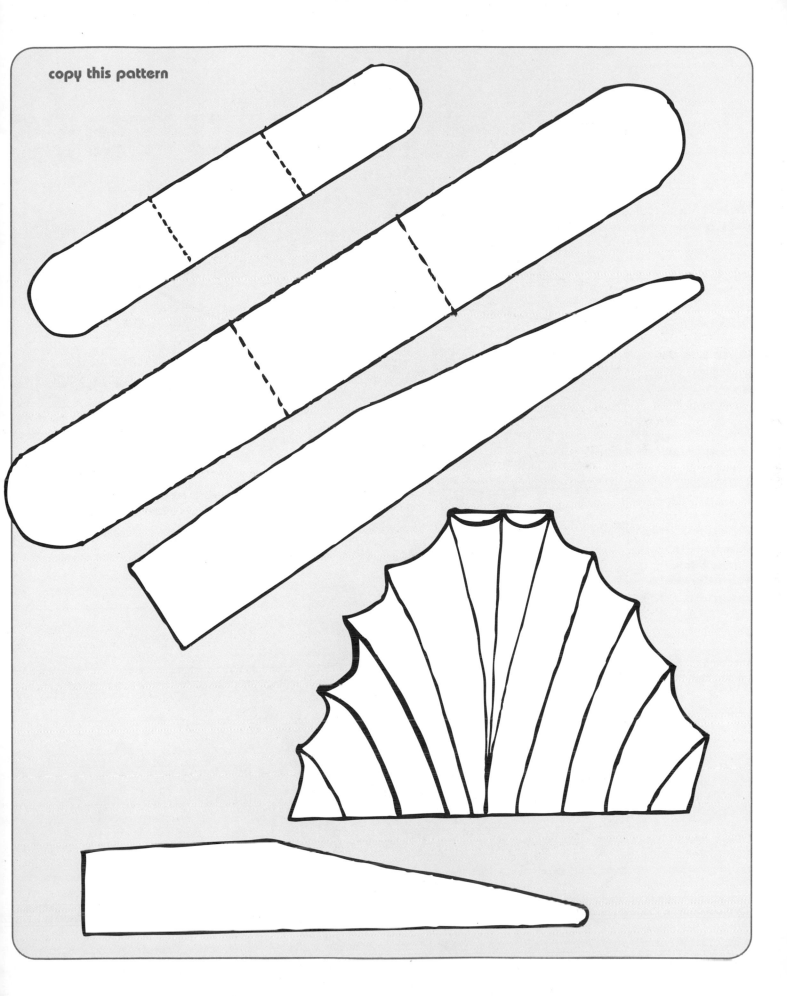

Lion and Lioness

Make two hand puppets of the king and queen of the jungle.

Ages:
Primary,
Intermediate,
Advanced

Materials for two puppets:
- *copy of patterns on page 76*
- *yellow, black, white, and brown construction paper*
- *ruler*
- *scissors*
- *white glue*
- *paper punch*
- *paper coffee filter*
- *water-base markers*
- *black pen or narrow marker*

1. Use the patterns to trace two yellow circle heads, four white eyes, two yellow tails, two brown noses, four yellow ears, four yellow front legs, and four yellow hind legs onto construction paper. Cut them out and set them aside.

2. To make the lion body, fold a sheet of yellow construction paper toward the center, 3 inches (7 1/2 centimeters) on each side. Overlap the back of the paper and glue the overlapping edges together. Also glue around the top of the head.

Fun Facts

- Male lions may be 10 feet (3 meters) long, including the tail. They can weigh 500 pounds (227 kilograms).

- In addition to roaring, lions also cough, growl, and grunt.

- A lion family is called a pride. It usually consists of two females and one male.

- Although a female lion (lioness) is smaller than the male, she does most of the hunting. After she catches dinner, she brings it to her mate and cubs.

- Newborn cubs have a spotted coat, which camouflages them as they hide in tall grass.

Hand Puppets

3. Trim the top to make it round like a mitten.

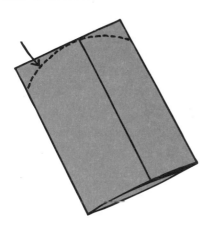

4. To make the male lion's mane, color a paper coffee filter with yellow, brown, black, and orange markers. Glue it onto the front of the puppet. Glue a yellow circle in the center of the coffee filter mane.

5. Glue on the ears, eyes, and nose as shown. Glue black paper punch dots on the eyes. Color the insides of the ears. Draw a mouth. Draw whisker dots.

6. Glue the front feet to the front of the puppet. Glue the back feet to the back so that they can be seen from the front.

7. Color the tip of the tail brown. Fringe it, using scissors. Glue on the lion tail so that it shows in front.

8. To make the lioness, repeat these steps, but do not glue on a mane.

Branching Out

- Write or record a story to act out with your lion puppets. Will you create a real story based on lion facts or a story about a pretend lion?

- Asian lions are protected in India in a wildlife sanctuary. Make a three-dimensional model of a wildlife sanctuary in which a lion might like to live.

- Lions were once found in Africa, Europe, and Asia but now live mainly in Africa, south of the Sahara Desert. The Sahara Desert is the largest desert in the world. Design a map of Africa, showing this desert.

Box Turtle Puppet

Make a box turtle puppet with a paper strip for your hand to hold onto.

**Ages:
Primary**

Materials for one box turtle:

- **copy of patterns on page 78**
- **construction paper**
- **scissors**
- **9-inch (23-centimeter) paper plate**
- **crayons**
- **colored tissue paper (optional)**
- **markers**
- **white glue**
- **paper punch**
- **paper fastener**
- **paper grocery bag**
- **stapler**

1. Use the patterns to trace a head, tail, and four feet onto construction paper. Draw eyes, mouth, and nostrils on the head. Draw claws on the feet. Cut them out and set them aside.

2. Color the bottom of the paper plate with crayons to look like a turtle shell, or glue on squares of colored tissue paper.

3. Punch a hole in the head and the shell. Fasten the head to the shell with a paper fastener as shown.

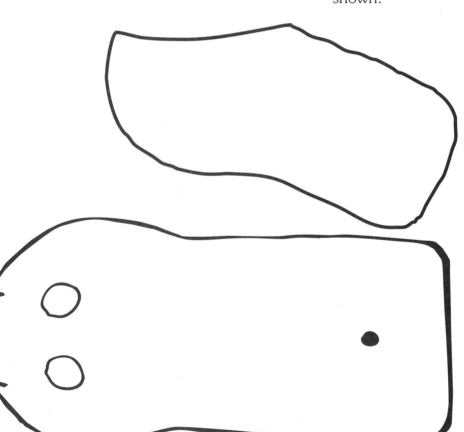

copy this pattern

Fun Facts

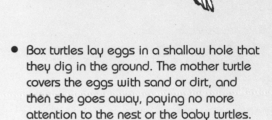

- Turtles have been on earth for at least 150 million years. About 250 different kinds of turtles can be found in most parts of the world.

- Some turtles are terrestrial; that is, they live on land. Others are aquatic; they live in the water.

- The box turtle is terrestrial. It lives in the United States and Mexico.

- Box turtles eat many things including earthworms, mushrooms, berries, tomatoes, snails, and insects.

- Box turtles lay eggs in a shallow hole that they dig in the ground. The mother turtle covers the eggs with sand or dirt, and then she goes away, paying no more attention to the nest or the baby turtles.

4. Glue on the feet and tail so they stick out from under the shell.

Branching Out

- Find out more about turtles around the world. Create another paper plate turtle by looking at turtle pictures and trying to copy the designs on the shells.

- Write a turtle poem or some reptilian spelling words under the shell of your puppet.

- Try writing a turtle play for your puppet.

5. To turn your turtle into a puppet, staple a strip of paper grocery bag, 2 × 11 inches (5 × 28 centimeters) long, under the shell.

6. Insert your hand between the strip and the shell, grasping the strip in your fist.

American Black

Make a black bear puppet with a puppet pocket for your hand.

Ages:
Primary,
Intermediate,
Advanced

Materials for one black bear puppet:
- **copy of patterns on page 82**
- **brown, black, and white construction paper**
- **scissors**
- **9-inch (23-centimeter) white paper plate**
- **stapler**
- **markers**
- **crayons**
- **white glue**

1. Use the patterns to trace a brown tail, two brown cheeks, two brown ears, two white eyes, a black nose, two brown front legs, and two brown hind legs onto construction paper. Cut them out and set them aside.

2. To make the body of the bear, use scissors to trim the sharp corners of a 9 × 12 inch (23 × 30$^1/_2$ centimeters) piece of brown construction paper.

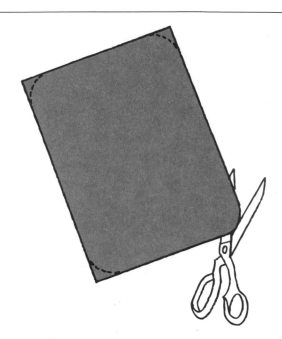

Fun Facts

- The American black bear may grow to be 6 feet (2 meters) long and weigh up to 500 pounds (227 kilograms).

- Black bears eat small animals, fish, berries, roots, insects, and grubs. Black bears love to visit campsites and will eat anything edible!

- The black bear is smart and can be taught tricks. Black bears have been known to unscrew jar lids to eat the jar's contents. Even if a black bear acts tame, it is always a wild animal and should be treated with distance and respect.

- Black bears hibernate in the winter. The female may have a litter of one to four cubs every two years.

Bear Puppet

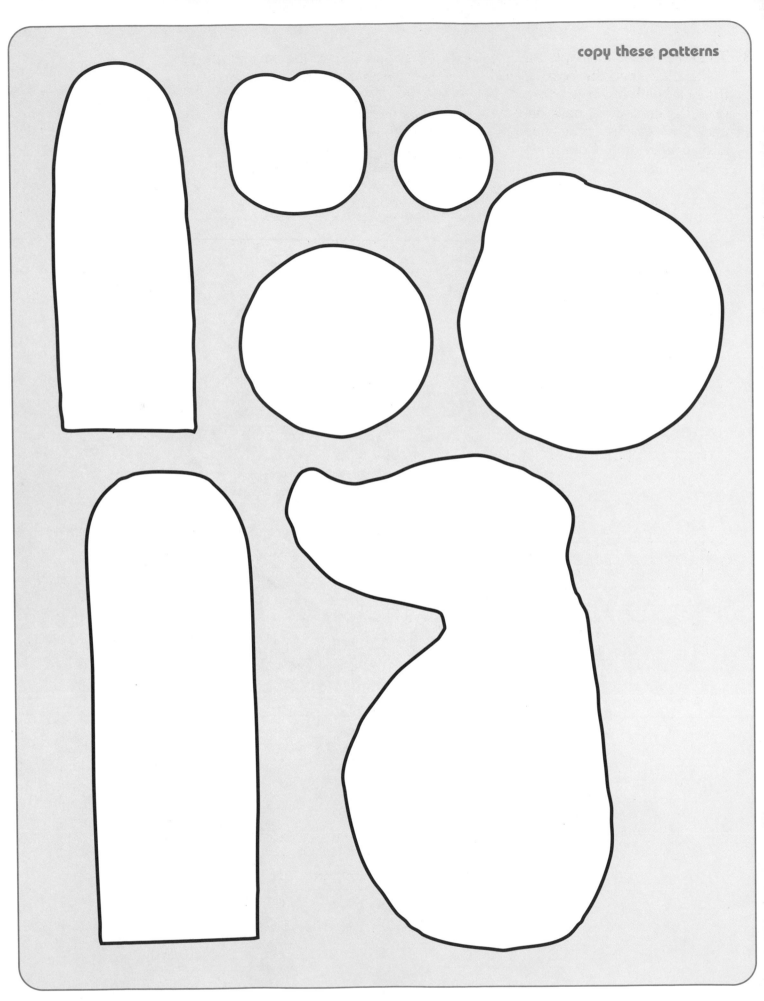

3. To make the head, staple the paper plate onto the body. Color the head with brown crayon. Glue the ears, eyes, nose, and cheeks as shown. Draw eyeballs and whisker dots. Color the inside of the ears.

4. Glue the tail onto the back of the body. Add the front and back paws.

5. Turn your bear into a puppet by adding a pocket to the back of the paper plate head. Use a half sheet of construction paper. Put glue around three edges, and stick it to the back of the head, creating an upside-down pocket of your hand.

Branching Out

- Bears are mammals. What is a mammal? What are some other wild and tame mammals?

- It is not a good idea to feed black bears that you see along the road or in parks. Can you find out why?

- Civilization has reduced the number and range of black bears. You can research the territory and status of this native American bear.

With the help of a string, this bluebird can flap its wings.

**Ages:
Intermediate,
Advanced**

Materials for one bluebird:
- copy of patterns on pages 86–87
- poster paper
- 9-inch (23-centimeter) white paper plate
- pencil
- scissors
- water–base markers
- crayons
- white glue
- stapler
- metal paper fastener
- 20-inch-long (51-centimeter-long) string

1. Trace the patterns for the bluebird body, wings, and tail onto poster paper. Cut them out.

2. Lay the patterns on the paper plate as shown. Draw around the patterns.

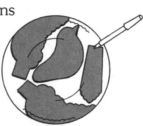

3. Color the bluebird wings, tail, head, and back with blue crayon. Color the chest with red crayon. Be sure to color both sides of your bird.

4. Cut out the bluebird pieces. Cut a slit in the bird's body as shown on the pattern.

5. The bluebird folds its feet under its body when flying. Draw feet under its wings.

6. Cut a slit in the tail and fold down the two tabs as shown on the pattern.

7. Slide the tail onto the back of the bluebird. Make a small hole through both tail tabs and the body, then insert a paper fastener.

8. Insert the two wings in the body slit. Overlap them and staple them together in the middle.

Fun Facts

- Eastern bluebirds and western bluebirds have red breasts and blue backs. The mountain bluebird is all blue.

- Bluebirds nest in holes in trees or fence posts. They will nest in a bird box if it is mounted low like a fence post.

Blue Bird

9. Make a small hole to insert the string in each wing as shown on the pattern. Tie one end of the string onto one wing and the other end of the string onto the other wing.

10. Hold the bird in one hand and lift up the middle of the string with the other hand to make your bluebird flap its wings.

Branching Out

- Write or dictate a story about your bluebird. What does it need to live a happy and healthy life?

- Ask an adult to help you build a bluebird nesting box.

copy these patterns

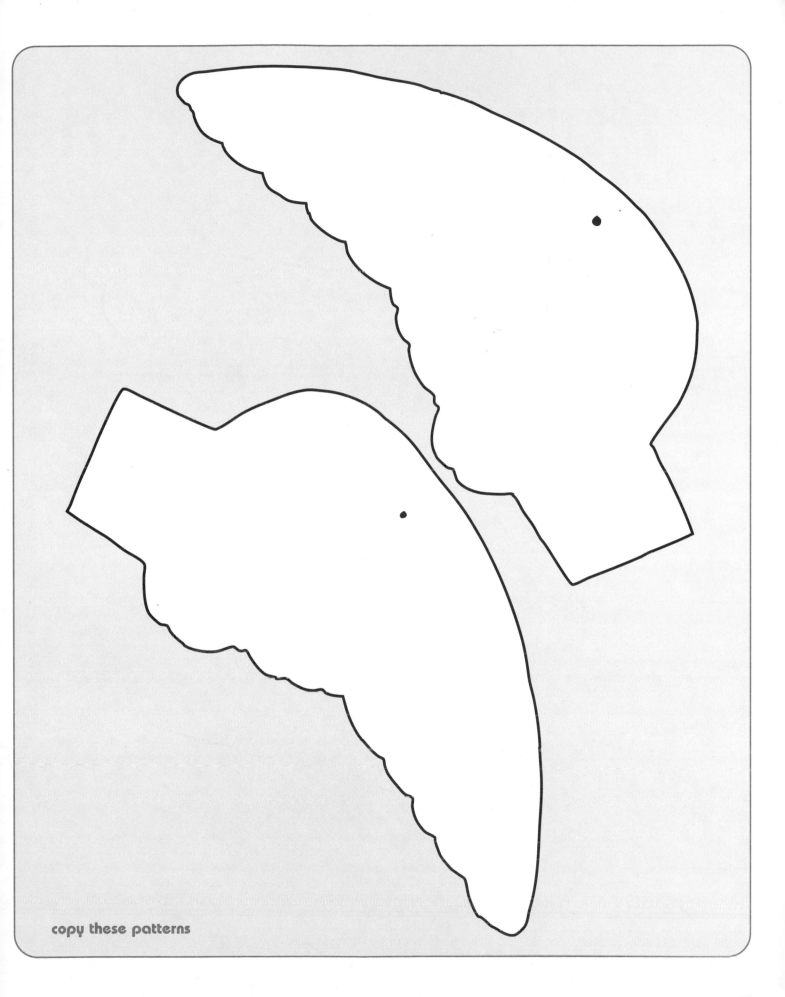

copy these patterns

Pteranodon, the

Make a pteranodon with wings that flap up and down.

**Ages:
Intermediate,
Advanced**

Materials for one pteranodon:
- **copy of patterns on pages 90–91**
- **poster paper**
- **markers**
- **crayons**
- **scissors**
- **white glue**
- **cardboard**

1. Use the patterns to trace the body, wings, feet, and midsection onto poster paper. Cut them out. An adult can make the cuts that are indicated on the patterns.

2. Cut two cardboard sticks $3/4 \times 7$ inches (2×18 centimeters) long.

3. Use crayons and markers to color all the pieces on both sides to look like a pteranodon.

4. Fasten the body to the underside of the wings by putting glue on Tabs A of the body. Glue the body to Points A in the middle of the wings. Glue the feet onto the wings at the X.

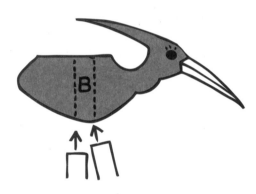

Fun Facts

- Fossils of the pteranodon have been found in Europe, Asia, and North America.

- Pteranodons had bodies about the size of a turkey. Their wings, however, were very large, usually about 25 feet ($7 1/2$ meters) across.

- Paleontologists believe that pteranodons built nests for hatching their eggs.

- In 1975, skeletons of three very large pteranodons were found in Big Bend National Park, Texas. The wingspan of the largest pteranodon was 51 feet ($15 1/2$ meters). It is by far the largest flying animal known.

- A pteranodon had a long pelican-like beak and no teeth. It probably ate fish.

Flying Reptile

5. Glue one end of each stick at Point B onto each side of the body. Then glue the sticks together down their full length. This creates a handle.

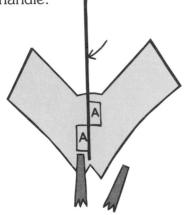

6. You have made a cut in the midsection. Push the end of the handle through this cut.

7. Push the midsection up to the pteranodon's body as far as it will go. Glue Tabs C to the underside of the wings at Points C.

8. Let the pteranodon dry upside down. To make the wings flap, hold the handle in one hand and move the midsection up and down with the other hand.

Branching Out

- Pteranodons are descendants of pterodactyls. They lived during the Cretaceous period of the Mesozoic Era. What other animals lived during this time? What must the world have looked like?

- Flying reptiles resembled birds in some ways. Can you discover ways in which flying reptiles and birds are alike and how they are different?

- Use the patterns for this pteranodon, change them by drawing and cutting, and create a new flying reptile. Is your version based on fact or fiction?

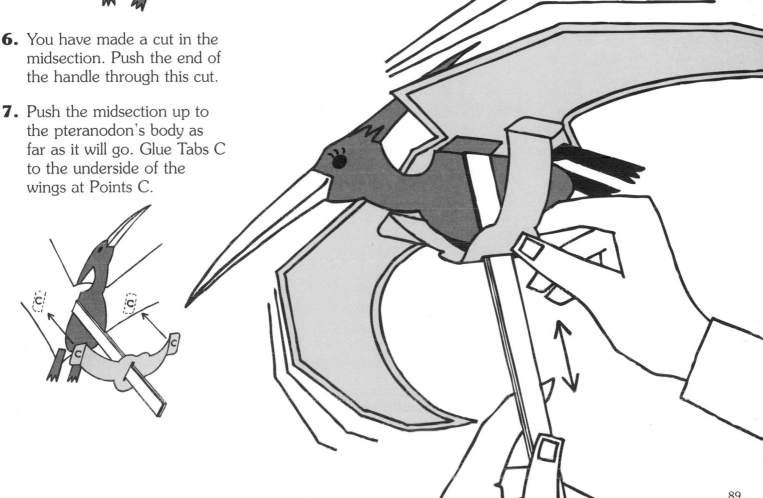

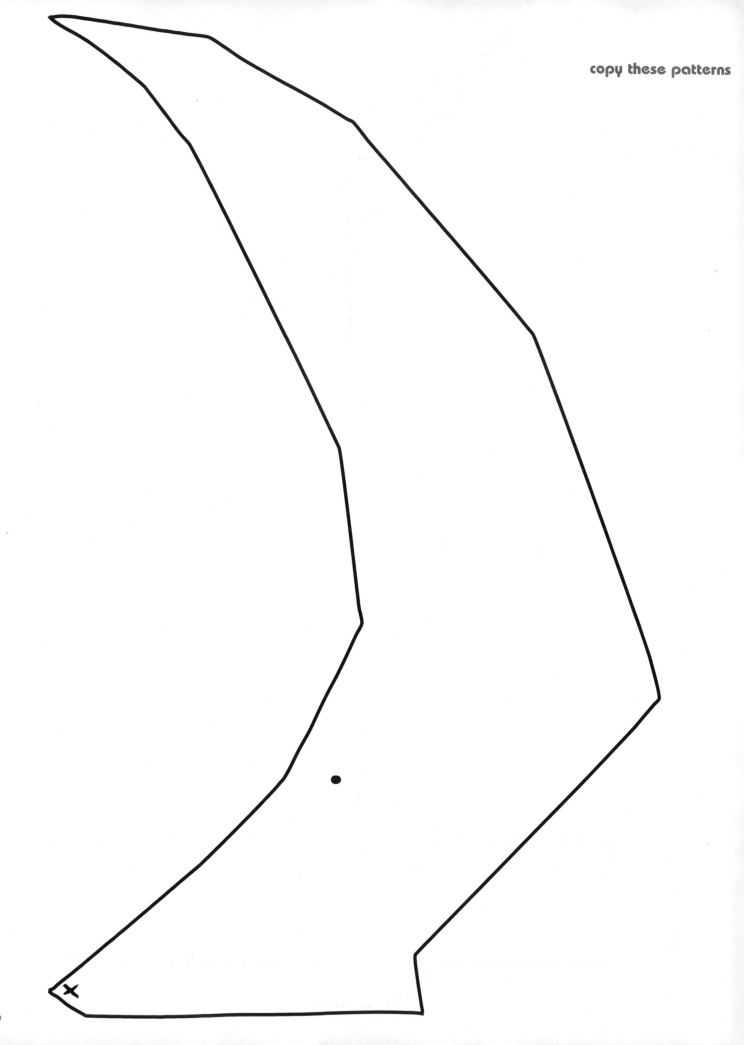

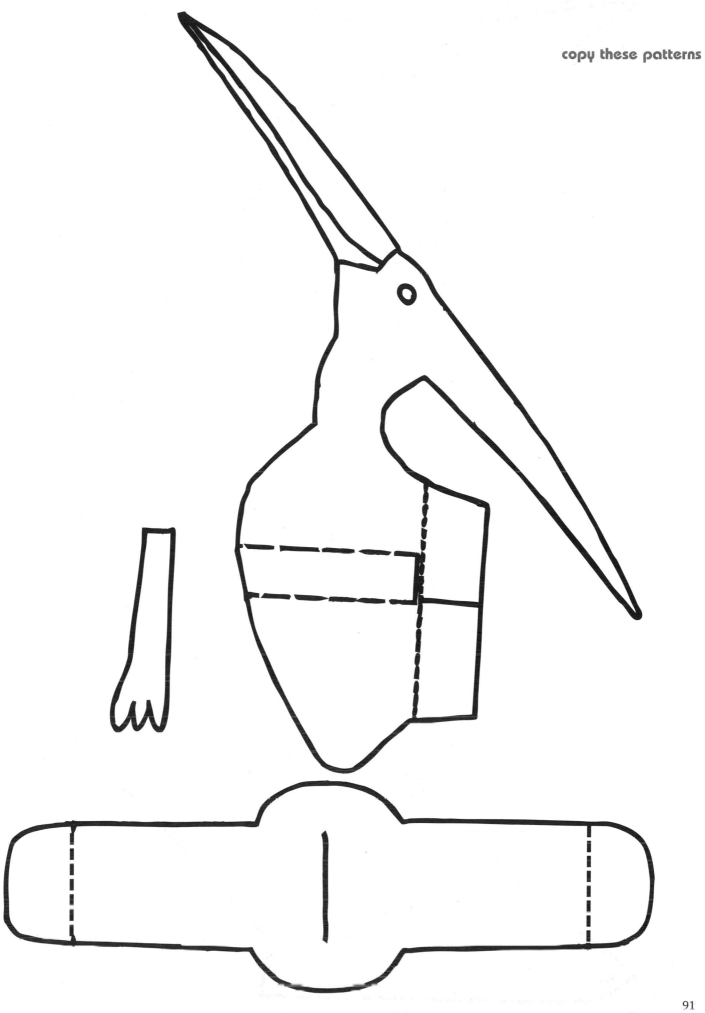

Make papier-maché Mars rocks that look like the ones photographed by the Mars robot car, Sojourner.

Ages:
*Primary,
Intermediate,
Advanced*

Materials for one Mars rock:
- *9-inch (23-centimeter) balloon*
- *1 1/2 cups (355 milliliters) flour*
- *1 cup (236 milliliters) water*
- *bowl*
- *wire whisk*
- *newspaper cut or torn into 1-inch-wide (2 1/2-centimeter-wide) strips*
- *brown tissue wrapping paper, cut into strips 1 x 3 inches (2 1/2 x 7 1/2 centimeters) long*

1. Blow up the balloon and tie a knot in the end.

2. Make papier-maché paste by mixing the flour and water in a bowl. Stir with the wire whisk to take out lumps. Make more if needed. A 5-pound (2.27-kilogram) bag of flour makes enough paste for about 25 moon rocks.

3. Tear the newspaper strips into 3-inch (7 1/2-centimeter) pieces.

4. Dip a strip into the paste. Gently pull the strip between your fingers to remove the extra paste. Smooth the strip onto the balloon.

5. Repeat this step until the entire balloon is covered, except for the end where it is knotted.

6. Cover the balloon with a second layer of paste strips. Make sure they are smooth.

Fun Facts

- Pathfinder, NASA's 3-foot-tall (91-centimeter-tall) spacecraft landed on Mars on July 4, 1997. It carried Sojourner, a robot car about the size of a laptop computer.

- Sojourner was designed to explore Mars' rocky terrain and investigate rocks all over the desert-like landing site. It is the first car to be driven on Mars.

- To get to Mars, Pathfinder travelled 310 million miles (500 million kilometers). The space voyage took seven months.

- Pathfinder weighed 1,256 pounds (570 kilograms). When it first entered Mars' atmosphere, it was travelling at 16,000 miles (26,715 kilometers) per hour. NASA engineers slowed its descent to only 22 miles (35.4 kilometers) per hour before it landed.

- A large parachute and a cocoon of balloons helped it land safely.

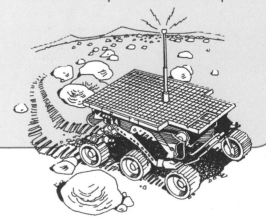

Mars Rocks

7. Now add a top layer of dry brown tissue paper strips. Put your Mars rock aside to dry for several days.

8. When it has completely dried, pop the balloon inside by cutting the tied end with scissors. Pull out the balloon and throw it away.

9. Close the hole in the rock with a few strips of newspaper dipped in papier-maché paste and a few strips of brown tissue paper. Let it dry a second time.

Branching Out

- NASA's scientists named the Mars rocks after cartoon characters, like Yogi and Casper. What would you like to name your Mars rock? Why did you choose that name?

- What can you find out about the two Viking missions to Mars in 1976?

- The Viking missions helped to make the 1997 landing on Mars successful. Can you find out some ways in which the two Viking missions contributed?

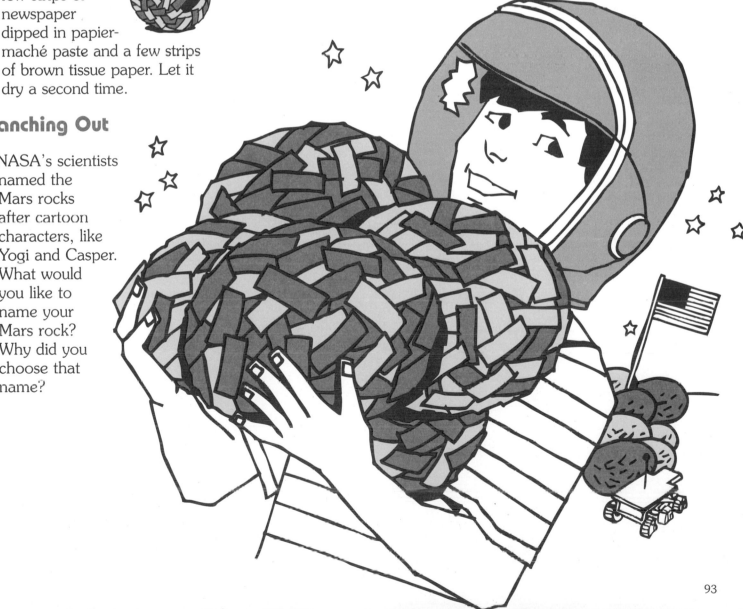

Bibliography

Craft Books and Resources

Adventures in Art: Art and Craft Experiences for 7- to 14-Year Olds by Susan Milord (Williamson, 1990). Intermediate and Advanced

Bags Are Big: A Paper Bag Craft Book by Nancy Renfro (Nancy Renfro Studios, 1986). All ages

Bio-Crafts is an Outdoor Biology Instructional Strategies (OBIS) module containing 9 activities that combine biology with arts and crafts. Available from Delta Education by calling 1-800-258-1302. Intermediate and Advanced

Crafts for Kids Who Are Wild About Dinosaurs, Crafts for Kids Who Are Wild About Insects, and Crafts for Kids Who Are Wild About Outer Space are by Kathy Ross (Millbrook Press, 1997). Primary and Intermediate

Easy Origami by Dokuohtei Nakano (Viking Penguin, 1994). Intermediate

EcoArt! Earth-Friendly Art and Craft Experiences for 3- to 9-Year Olds by Laurie Carlson (Williamson, 1993). Primary and Intermediate

Fun Factory: Games and Toys from Household Junk by Lindsay Milne (Reader's Digest Kids, 1995). Intermediate and Advanced

Kid Style Nature Crafts: 50 Terrific Things To Make With Nature's Materials by Gwen Diehn and Terry Krautwurst (Sterling, 1995). Advanced

Kidpix is a software package that helps kids draw, paint, and animate. Broderbund, 1-800-423-9999. All ages

Kids Create! Art and Craft Experiences for 3- to 9-Year-Olds by Laurie Carlson (Williamson, 1990). Primary and Intermediate

My Nature Craft Book by Cheryl Owen (Little, Brown & Co., 1993). All ages

My Very First Nature Craft Book by Anna Curti (Simon & Schuster, 1996). Primary

Puddles and Wings and Grapevine Swings by Imogene Forte and Marjorie Frank (Incentive Publications, 1982). All ages

Snips and Snails and Walnut Whales by Phyllis Fiorotta (Workman, 1975). All ages

Natural Resources

Ranger Rick, *published by the National Wildlife Federation, is a monthly nature magazine for elementary-age children.*

Ranger Rick® magazine is an excellent source of additional information and activities on many other aspects of nature, outdoor adventure, and the environment. This 48-page award-winning monthly publication of the National Wildlife Federa-tion is packed with the highest-quality color photos, illustrations, and both fiction and nonfiction articles. All factual information in **Ranger Rick** has been checked for accuracy by experts in the field. The articles, games, puzzles, photo-stories, crafts, and other features inform as well as entertain and can easily be adapted for classroom use. To order or for more information, call 1-800-588-1650.

The EarthSavers Club provides an excellent opportunity for you and your students to join thousands of others across the country in helping to improve our environment. Sponsored by Target Stores and the National Wildlife Federation, this program provides children aged 6 to 14 and their adult leaders with free copies of the award-winning **EarthSavers** newspaper and **Activity Guide** four times during the school year, along with a leader's handbook, EarthSavers Club certificate, and membership cards. For more information on how to join, call 1-703-790-4535 or write to EarthSavers; National Wildlife Federation; 8925 Leesburg Pike; Vienna, VA 22184.